ESCORT-IN-CHIEF

Foreword by

PROF LUKOYE ATWOLI

ESCORT-IN-CHIEF

Through the Eyes of a Physician

DR BUNDI KARAU

This memoir is a work of creative nonfiction reflecting the author's recollections of their experiences as a physician. While the author shares their journey, offering insight and, sometimes, raising awareness, it is not intended to provide medical advice or replace the guidance of qualified healthcare professionals. The author's experiences are unique, and what worked for them may not be suitable for others. Please consult with your doctor or other healthcare provider for any health concerns or before making any decisions related to your medical care.

The author has taken great care to alter the stories and circumstances to conceal the identities of the patients described in this book. Names of individuals explicitly mentioned were used with their permission, and others were changed.

ISBN: 978-9914-9491-8-6

Kindle Edition, by Mystery Books, an imprint of Mystery Publishers – 2025

Paperback Edition

Published by:
Mystery Publishers Limited
P.O. BOX 18016 – 20100
Tel: +254 718 429 184
Nakuru, Kenya
Email: publishing@mysterypublisherslimited.com
www.mysterypublisherslimited.com

Cover design by Vincent De Paul
Typeset in PT Serif pt.11 by Mystery Publishers Limited

Available from Amazon and other online retail outlets, Kindle and other devices, and bookstores in Kenya.

For:

The three most important women in my life: the one who gave me the love for storytelling, the one who brought me forth and up, and the one who escorts me in the journey of life—my grandmother, the late Lucia Kathang'a Ĩtũrĩu; my mother Joyce Mbaa Karau, and my wife, Dr Winnie Mueni Saumu-Bundi.

CONTENTS

FOREWORD

FEW ACTS ARE MORE VITAL to medicine's soul than telling its stories. In *Escort-in-Chief: Through the Eyes of a Physician*, Dr Bundi Karau has offered us not only a chronicle of clinical encounters but a deeply human narrative that bridges the gap between the science of medicine and the art of healing.

Due to the nature of our work, doctors stand at the crossroads of life's most profound moments—hope and despair, suffering and recovery, life and death. Yet, too often, the richness of these experiences remains locked away, unspoken, or lost to the relentless pace of our profession. When we, as physicians, take the time to write our stories, we do more than preserve memories; we create a living archive of wisdom, empathy, and reflection.

Writing allows us to process the dilemmas and emotions we face—moral, ethical, and personal—and to find meaning in our daily encounters. It is a therapeutic act that demonstrates our humanity and helps us understand ourselves and our patients more deeply.

Dr Karau's work is a testament to the power of narrative. He writes not only to inform but to connect—to make the world of medicine accessible and relatable to all. His stories are not cloaked in jargon or detached clinical observation. They are vivid, honest, and humble accounts that invite readers into the lived reality of a physician's journey. In doing so, he honours the tradition of medical storytellers who came before us, whose words have shaped both our understanding of disease and our sense of what it means to care.

Storytelling in medicine serves many purposes. It enhances our communication with patients, making complex diagnoses and treatments understandable and memorable. It inspires trust, builds rapport, and motivates both patients and colleagues. Writing is part of the communication skills we must master to better understand the travails of those who come to us for support and to communicate back to them our understanding of their suffering and our plans to help alleviate it.

For those in training, stories offer lessons that textbooks cannot, often illustrating the nuances of care, the challenges of uncertainty, and the necessity of resilience. For our communities, these narratives humanise the statistics of illness and health, shedding light on disparities and advocating for change.

Most importantly, writing in a relatable manner, as Dr Karau has so masterfully done, ensures that our stories are not just heard but also felt. They reach beyond the walls of the clinic or hospital, touching the hearts of patients, families, and fellow professionals alike. By sharing his journey, Dr Karau reminds us that every patient, every victory, and every defeat is a story worth telling—a story that can teach, heal, and inspire.

Hopefully, this book will encourage more physicians to pick up the pen to reflect and to share. Our profession, our patients, and our own well-being will be the richer for it.

Lukoye Atwoli
MBChB, MMed Psych, PhD, *MBS, MKNAS*
Professor in Psychiatry and
Dean Medical College East Africa;
Deputy Director, Brain and Mind Institute
The Aga Khan University

Nairobi, April 2025

PREFACE

WRITING IS THE MOST POWERFUL means of impacting lives. We know about great historical figures like Isaac Newton, William Shakespeare, and Paul of Tarsus not because of what they said (they might have said many great things) but because of their writings. Hundreds of years from now, future generations will be able to imagine how we lived, what we accomplished and the challenges we faced from what we write. They will reflect on their own lives and, in turn, on their own future through the prism of our writing.

A physician's encounter with a patient is supposed to be a private matter. But such an encounter can be used creatively to educate, rebuke, inform and even entertain. Every patient, every disease, every symptom is a story in itself. The vivid descriptions of diseases in the past allowed us to diagnose these conditions. When James Parkinson wrote 'An Essay on the

Shaking Palsy' in 1817, he was sharing his thoughts not only with the medical community. He was writing for posterity. Through his description, we are mesmerised by his approach and meticulousness. We learn how, long before the advent of complicated laboratory and imaging tests, the physician was able to deal with the great challenges of the day.

Perhaps the first description of Myasthenia gravis, a disease that causes muscle weakness on exercise, is the description of the travails of a Native American chief, Opechancanough.

> "
>
> *ıe excessive fatigue he encountered wrecked his constitution; his flesh became macerated; his sinews lost their tone and elasticity; and his eyelids were so heavy that he could not see unless they were lifted up by his attendants . . . he was unable to walk; but his spirit rising above the ruins of his body directed from the litter on which he was carried by his Indians.*

The writings of Dr Yves Rosendo Ribeiro shed light on a nascent Nairobi City, the epidemiology of the disease in that era, and how, almost barehanded, he summoned the courage to fight an epidemic. He writes of his struggle between modern medicine and cultural practices and how these collided, often with lethal consequences, in an emerging city. We learn not only medicine from his writings, but also our origins, our beginnings and our struggles.

Advancements in medicine came out of the poetic writings of these ancient medical practitioners.

We certainly have not reached the end of medical discoveries. New diseases continue to emerge, and old diseases continue to present in strange, hitherto unknown ways. This means our writing today may well inform the discoveries of tomorrow.

Above all, this book is a chronicle of my encounters. It tells the story of what ails us, how we respond to it, where we succeed and where we fail.

I welcome you.

Dr Bundi Karau
(BSc, MBChB, MMed. Internal Medicine, PhD, Fellowship [Neurol]);
Consultant Physician and Clinical Neuroscientist

ACKNOWLEDGEMENTS

I WISH TO CONVEY MY heartfelt thanks to my wife, Dr Winnie Mueni Saumu-Bundi, for being quietly by my side since our first year of medical school, her constant encouragement, companionship and above all, her love.

Under the watchful tutelage of my brother, Dr Muriira Karau, I learnt how to thread my first sentences and tell a story. Decades later, he remains a constant source of encouragement and support. I thank him most sincerely.

My great friend and sister, Jerusha Kananu Marete, called me out of the blue three years ago and insisted that I had a story to tell. When I asked her which one, she told me that my life, every patient I encountered, and every victory and defeat as a physician is a story to be told. I'm grateful to her for nudging me ahead and always exhorting me that one sentence gives rise to a paragraph and, eventually, a story. She was presciently right.

If storytelling is indeed a gift passed down from ancestors, I must thank my late grandmother, Lucia Kathang'a Ĩtũrĩu (1915-2012), who instilled in me a love for a good story. Of all her descendants, I might have inherited this trait from her. Not only did she pass it through genes, but I also saw her in her element of storytelling, embellishing every encounter and deriving great pleasure in narration. Even in her death, she is fondly remembered and appreciated.

I sincerely thank Governor Kiraitu Murungi for placing his trust in me.

During my last round of training, which took me to Bangalore, India, fate and God enabled me to meet with a man who became a mentor and a friend. I thank Professor Thomas Mathew for his mentorship, passion for teaching, and passion for God, which he rubbed onto me.

I thank all those who gave me permission to use their real names in this book for accepting to be part of this story.

Finally, I thank God for the gift of energy and passion—teaching, treating patients, motivating, and even writing. All these require unlimited reserves of motivation and energy, which I believe are endowed to me by my creator.

INTRODUCTION

A PHYSICIAN'S CALLING

TO WORK AS A PHYSICIAN is, in essence, to escort people through life's journey. The journey of life is perilous, tumultuous and full of uncertainty. There comes a time when you need a steady hand to guide, encourage and support you in life.

The physician plays the role of escort-in-chief, dispelling worry and fear, reassuring, chaperoning and eventually delivering the human to the Maker. The physician must ultimately fail in their work if they consider it their job to prevent death because death must come. It is, therefore, not the primary duty of the physician to keep off death. Their role is to provide certainty while trying to avert preventable and premature death. As such, a physician is the choirmaster in life's orchestra.

While a young doctor, I revelled in clinching difficult diagnoses. Today, my joy is in securing the trust of my people and making them feel healthy and secure. Thus, when a friend hands me their 90-year-old father to take care of, I know they don't expect me to avert death. Rather, they expect me to provide comfort, hope and companionship in the sunset of life.

Given this primal role, a physician must be humble. Nothing humbles more than knowing how the body works. Nothing humbles more than knowing that, despite all the knowledge, the body will fall apart someday. A physician must be accommodating. Patients present with symptoms that are often incredulous, sometimes bizarre, and at other times annoying. It is his work to separate the wheat from the chaff and provide clarity to the patient.

A physician must never tire of seeing their patients attended to properly. They must reach out to other specialities and become the choir conductor, even if they can't sing all the notes. They must know who can sing which note and where they can be found. They must endeavour to point the patient in that direction.

Sometimes, stress is our companion because of the things we see. But a physician must never give up hope. For, when soldiers raise their hands in surrender in the face of an invader, what are the citizens to do? The physician will stay on the frontline, at their own risk, even to death. We witnessed this ultimate sacrifice during the COVID-19 pandemic. We witness it daily from physicians who contract tuberculosis, suffer needle stick injuries, and other exposures.

A physician must learn to be simple in approach but never simplistic in thinking. They must digest test results and physical exam findings and present the information to the patient or caregiver in clear, understandable terms. A physician must keep reading, for there's nothing linear in medicine. I recently saw a colleague almost die of malaria. Certainly not the malaria I read in medical school—her presentation was not classic at all.

A physician must form a personal philosophy which guides them in their approach to disease. My philosophy is that a patient is a whole being, and all aspects must be handled with care. I would not be succeeding as a physician if I controlled elevated blood pressure and left the patient with erectile dysfunction. It has also been my philosophy that when no diagnosis is apparent, tuberculosis remains a possibility and must be treated. I have had heated discussions with public health officials over this, and I always win when that emaciated patient suddenly gets back to her feet and starts gaining weight.

To sit at the centre of the music of life and to be able to shepherd lives through the ravages of life is an honour I cherish. Every waking day, I endeavour to be that physician who listens, touches, reassures, comforts and gently instructs.

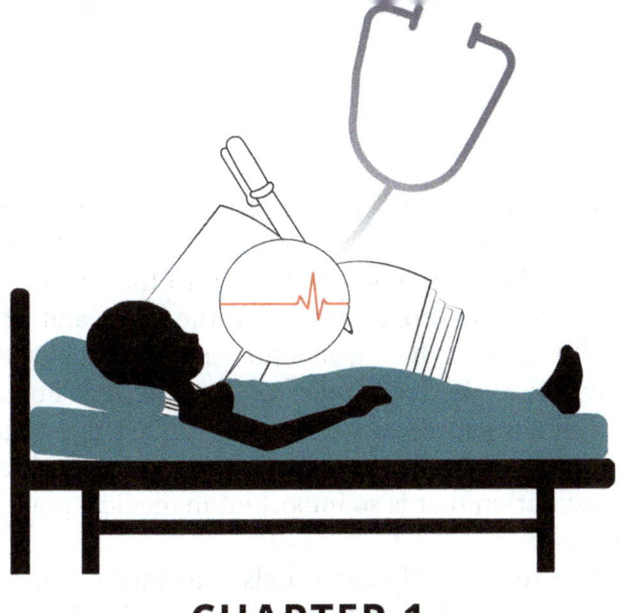

CHAPTER 1

THE BEGINNINGS

THE FIRST YEAR OF MEDICAL school has always been daunting for those joining the profession. Apart from the large volumes of books one has to consume, it is also the year when a new medical language is learnt and henceforth applied in all aspects of medical education and practice. Terms such as *medial*, *lateral*, *caudal*, *distal*, and a whole lot of Latin, Greek, and 'medicalese' for common body structures are learnt—and form part of the cult of medicine that can communicate without the uninitiated knowing what is being said.

It is also the year learners are introduced to their first 'patient', the cadaver. This dead human body is devoured from the buttocks down to the sole of the foot, from the shoulder down to the hand, and from the head, neck, thorax, abdomen and, eventually, the pelvis in a year-long frenzy of learning that imbues the budding medical student with knowledge of the anatomy of the human body and the hand–brain coordination that is so important in medical practice later on.

The tough initiation rituals into medical school have been handed down over the centuries. They are practised with the same zeal and sternness, perhaps to scare away jokers who would want to be doctors. It is also a way to preserve the sanctity of what is labelled a noble profession.

I was in the middle of my first year of medical school when I had an encounter that changed my perspective. Two years before, in 2003, I had proudly announced that I wanted to become a pathologist. Having topped the nation in the Kenya Certificate of Secondary Education (KCSE), journalists flocked to my former high school eager to hear if this 'village boy' knew what he wanted with his life.

"Pathology deals mostly with dead bodies. Are you not afraid of this?" Asked one journalist.

"Nothing in medicine is a bed of roses," I nonchalantly asserted. Not that I knew much about medicine, aside from the infatuation we had with careers and the pride I felt when I first read of the exploits of Ben Carson, a neurosurgeon in the USA.

Nonetheless, I will confess that my infatuation with pathology, and the major driving force to become a doctor, was instilled in me by the characters of Aoro and Wandia in the book *The River and the Source*. The exploits of Wandia, who went on to become a professor of pathology, captured my imagination. The enduring testimony of how books can shape the minds of children is borne by my career choice and even the choice of my future spouse.

On 22 June 2005, midway through the daunting first year of medical school, near-tragedy struck in my life. I woke up in the middle of the night with a crushing abdominal pain. For a few minutes, I ignored the pain, but the intensity increased. I started sweating profusely, and within no time, I experienced trouble breathing. I tried to arouse my cube-mate, who was snoring away in bed.

'Prefabs', the wooden houses where we found ourselves accommodated by the University of Nairobi, had small rooms that could only fit a bed, a small wardrobe, and a reading table. A hardboard separated the next room, and you could easily jump over. I shouted to Peter, a dental surgery student who lived in the next room. Together with Wagura Karuga, his cube-mate, they swung into action and started the dash down the hill to the university's Student and Staff Hospital.

Peter thrust me on his back, thanks in no small part to my small frame, and ran as fast as he could while Wagura followed hot in pursuit. Peter kept saying, *"Mtoto ni mgonjwa sana"*, calling me a child despite the fact that we were all first-year university students.

We reached the hospital across State House Road and met a gentleman who clearly didn't like his job.

"Young man, you are one of these people who go drinking, and then you come to disturb us at night, eh?" He asked with a menacing voice.

I didn't have the energy to reply, for I was half dead. I have never tasted alcohol in my life, and the closest encounter with it is the smell from a pub as I pass by.

He didn't even enquire much as he had already formed an opinion. He didn't examine me. He gave us a few tablets, and we returned to Mamlaka Hostels, where we lived.

I had hardly swallowed the pills when my two friends noticed my condition was worsening.

We rushed back, astride Peter's back, to the hospital. The doctor who had, moments earlier, dismissed us, sprinted towards us just as my friends deposited me on the floor.

"Move!" he barked, dropping to his knees beside me. He pressed two fingers to the carotid artery. "Get the ambulance!" he shouted.

I was writhing in pain, and the doctor seemed to be losing it. I began to lose consciousness just as a siren wailed in the distance. I felt myself being lifted and placed somewhere, and as I swam in the delirium, I spotted the doctor in that foggy image, guilt clawing at his chest. I heard beeping monitors and the medics' terse commands. When I lost consciousness completely, the last image was of the doctor's pale face, perhaps praying that wherever the ambulance was taking me could undo what his arrogance had set in motion.

I woke up to feel a doctor poking my tummy with a needle. I tensed my abdominal muscles as he muttered some words and pushed the needle on the right side of the umbilicus. I winced in pain. After plunging the needle into my tummy, he pulled back to aspirate, but nothing came out. I heard him mention 'ascites', but these were just words to me. I did not understand what ascites meant. Only later did I know that he was alluding to the collection of fluid within the abdomen.

The hospital corridors looked menacing and deathly, and the only sounds I could hear as I lay on the cold couch were the humming and beeping of life support machines and the interrupted sounds of wailing by relatives. I interpreted every round of wailing to mean that a life had been lost. I was terrified.

I was at Kenyatta National Hospital and was admitted to Ward 8A. I tried to engage the nurse who came to administer an intravenous drip about what I was being treated for. He curtly asked me to direct the question to the doctors when they came for the ward round.

The next morning, a group of doctors appeared in the room I shared with an elderly man. It did not occur to me that most of them were undergraduate medical students, a few residents in internal medicine, and the consultant physician.

I remember one of the medical students palpating my abdomen under the stern gaze of the physician. Once in a while, he would be interrupted by the senior.

"Young man, you seem to have forgotten your basic anatomy."

"I will send you back to Chiromo for a month of re-education in anatomy!" (Chiromo is the campus of the University of Nairobi, where first- and second-year medical students, also known as preclinical students, undertake their basic science courses.)

The ward round crew left my room, but my mind buzzed with questions and worry. I heard words like cancer, pancreatitis, tuberculosis, perforated duodenal ulcer and peritonitis, but nobody would tell me what I was suffering from. The pain had reduced in intensity, but I felt my abdomen heavy and dull. I had been asked not to take any meal, what the medics call *nil per oral*.

I called Biribwa, one of the final-year undergraduate students who was in the round and appeared more friendly and asked him what I was suffering from. He promised to look at my file. Biribwa, today a prominent plastic and reconstructive surgeon, later became a lifelong friend. He kept coming to check on me. According to the file, no diagnosis of my abdominal pain had been established. However, he noted that I was on metronidazole and ceftriaxone, antibiotics, which meant that I might have had an infection somewhere.

Subsequent ward rounds were quicker and more dismissive. The resident would give a quick summary of my condition, and they would move on to the next patient. Once in a while, the consultant in the round would throw a question, which was met by silence as he looked around. He would then urge the residents and students to read deeper.

As I recuperated in Ward 8A, I began receiving large groups of my classmates from Chiromo, who would spend most evenings by my side, sharing jokes and stories and eventually praying for me. It was deeply touching.

***

A few months before, when we had reported to Chiromo to begin our medical training, I had struck a friendship with a girl to whom I felt attracted. We became good friends and would share messages and calls.

At the beginning of June 2005, we had a two-week break, the only break of the gruelling forty-four weeks of the first year of our training. I found myself sharing texts and almost daily calls with this girl.

In one of the messages, she wrote, *"Je t'aime,* Bundi." Perhaps due to naivety, I did not bother to find out the meaning of the French words. Only after we resumed the session, a few days before the illness, did I share the words with Wagura. He burst out laughing.

"*Kijana unapendwa!"* He blurted out.

"No way. I would be foolish to fall in love this early in our training!" I declared.

"Can we bet?" A scheming Peter, his cubemate, chimed in.

"Yes!"

Peter fished out a piece of paper on which we had declared that I, Bundi, would not fall in love with any girl until I had finished my medical degree and attained a PhD. In turn, Peter and Wagura declared that I would date a girl before I finished the first year of our course. We promised that either party would pay the other five thousand Kenya shillings if the bet materialised.

Deep inside, I knew that I loved this girl. But being a man, I had to feign disinterest. I was, after all, the best candidate in the country for the 2002 Kenya Certificate of Secondary Education (KCSE), and I had to project an aura of seriousness in my studies, not being swayed by small matters of love.

I need not say that I dated the girl before the end of our first year in medical school, much to the delight of Peter and Wagura. But it is this illness that watered the seed of love. The strengthened relationship endured six years of medical school and blossomed into a marriage.

This illness also planted the seed of my love for internal medicine. Even in the face of uncertain illness, I saw a need for decisiveness, clarity, empathy and better communication. And I knew that was my calling.

I was eventually discharged after ten days to continue receiving my injections at the university sanatorium. I had fully recovered. The diagnosis remained a mystery, but having recovered, neither I nor the doctors were interested in knowing what ailed me. They had fired a missile in darkness that hit the target. They didn't need to know how the target took that position.

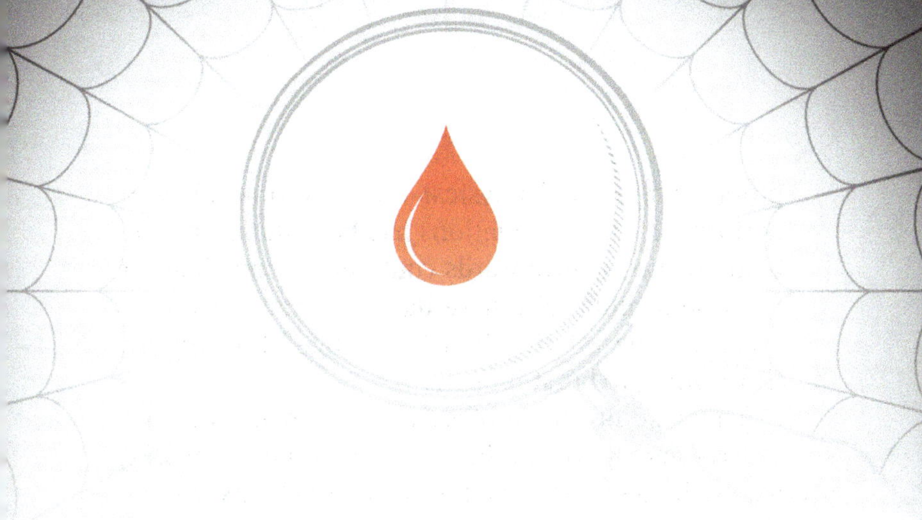

CHAPTER 2

THE JUNGLE

"MEDICINE IS A JUNGLE," SAID one of our senior professors to a stunned audience during one of the famous grand rounds at Kenyatta National Hospital. After a moment's silence that seemed like an eternity, he added, for good measure, "And I'm the king of the jungle."

The undergraduate medical students gathered in the sloping hallway burst into suppressed laughter. The statement had followed a gruelling discussion in which a resident presented a case of a patient with ascites for which no diagnosis could be made. A proper history and physical examination had been performed. All investigations had been done. Yet, the team in the medical wards could not do much apart from performing alternate-day *therapeutic paracentesis*, tapping off the fluid that bulged the tummy, threatening to burst it open.

The gist of the professor's statement was not exactly metaphorical in the way a jungle works, where there's no law and the strongest claims the kill. He meant that some medical cases were so confusing and confounding that sifting through the jungle of medical history, examination, and diagnostic tests required a real king. Where surgery requires hand-brain coordination, internal medicine requires the astuteness of a chess player. You think a few steps in advance, start simple and then launch into complicated attacks to overwhelm the opponent.

It is more like a detective. Not only do you need a keen eye, but you also must possess the audacity to make the moves and follow them through. Team play becomes critical because of the labyrinthine anatomy and physiology of the human body. The most confounding thing is that even your juniors can end up with the decisive move that clinches the diagnosis. The diagnosis is not an end in itself; management must be coordinated.

The professor's statement made little practical sense until I qualified as a physician and moved back to practice in the district.

I received a call about a seventy-year-old gentleman with anaemia whose cause remained a mystery. The case immediately roused my attention. Every time I led the major ward round at Meru Teaching and Referral Hospital, I would encourage my juniors to strive to determine the cause of anaemia, always reminding them that anaemia is not a diagnosis in itself. So many patients with anaemia of 'undetermined cause' pass through the public healthcare system. Oftentimes, they are transfused and discharged, only to come back a few weeks or months later with symptomatic anaemia.

I scheduled the old man for an appointment and asked him to come in with his wife and bring all his medical records.

Observing his steps as he opened the door, I could see fatigue and a sense of discouragement in the way he walked, took a seat and spoke. His name was Geoffrey.

"I'm already tired of transfusion. What exactly is happening, doctor?" He asked in a frustrated voice.

The practice of internal medicine requires patience. The patience to ask and answer even the mundane questions. The patience and keenness to pick the subtlest of clues. The patience to leaf through pages of investigations. The patience to refer to or consult colleagues. And the courage to accept when you don't know.

This man had battled anaemia for five months. It started with a dizzying feeling that made him zone out for a few seconds. On this occasion, his haemoglobin was found to be at a critical three (the normal being above twelve). He had been promptly admitted and given four transfusions. When his haemoglobin rose to eight, he was released. And thence began his arduous journey to find an elusive diagnosis.

I steadied myself and decided to start from the beginning: a proper and detailed history. He had no chronic disease before this problem. He had no bleeding diathesis. He could not tell whether his stool was black, what we call *melaena stool*. He had not seen blood in the stool. His urine was straw-coloured. He ate iron-rich foods. He did not consume herbal concoctions or any drugs that could cause gastritis. He had no dyspepsia. He had no bone pains. He had no bleeding gums. He had no recurrent fevers. I asked all the questions I thought could help me identify at least one risk factor or cause to hold on to. None was forthcoming.

I laid him on the couch. He was pale. His gums were pale but not overgrown. He had no hint of jaundice. He had no enlarged lymph nodes, and the spleen and liver were not palpable. His deep tendon reflexes were intact.

Having satisfied myself that his haematological evaluation did not reveal any clues apart from pallor, I asked for his records, which he had neatly arranged in a folder. I looked at his blood counts, which were done in various clinics and hospitals. They showed low haemoglobin. The white blood cells and platelets were within normal limits. The red blood cell indices indicated microcytic anaemia, a condition that is often explained by blood loss, low iron intake, or some inborn anomalies. His upper and lower gastrointestinal endoscopies did not reveal any tumours, ulcers or signs of bleeding. He had an abdominal CT scan that concluded that his abdomen was normal.

He had a guaiac test that was positive, an indicator that he could be losing blood from the stomach or intestines. But again, the sensitivity of this test threw doubt in my mind.

To extricate myself from this situation and give myself room to think, I requested his admission for further transfusion and more tests. He was not amused that we needed more tests when, in his view, we had done 'scanning of almost the whole body'. I politely explained to him that there was still more ground to cover.

When ordering investigations, physicians will choose either a series or parallel method of investigation. The series method is preferred where resources are limited and where there's adequate time, for it advocates performing one test after the other in a logical sequence. The parallel method, favoured by the rich, advocates performing all tests in one go and then filtering through them to make sense of the diagnosis. It is preferred where finances are not a problem, the fear of litigation is rife, and diagnosis is urgent.

I explained to Geoffrey that we would adopt the series method and illustrated the sequence we would follow, as well as the anticipated costs, on a piece of paper.

Sitting at the helm of medicine in a district is an advantage as well as a disadvantage. The advantage lies in the fact that patients coming to you have already covered some ground in terms of diagnostic investigations. All you need to do is determine which few steps to take to the final. It is much like being the last runner in a relay where your team has already opened a wide lead. All you must do is increase the tempo and romp into victory. The disadvantage is that patients are already tired and disillusioned by their contact with the healthcare system. You must also bear the brunt of making the final diagnosis, breaking bad news, and planning the ultimate management.

In Geoffrey's case, I had the advantage of substantial ground having been covered in his diagnostic journey. But I still felt apprehensive.

We began by ordering serum iron investigations and a bone marrow aspirate. Thanks to cooperative relatives, the results were out in a few days. I sensed a sliver of light on the horizon. It was confirmed that his serum iron stores were critically low. The bone marrow aspirate did not yield much except for depleted marrow iron stores.

Confident that we were dealing with a case of blood loss, I convinced them that we needed to repeat the endoscopies. Maybe with better preparation, we could pinpoint the source of blood loss. Geoffrey looked sceptical, but his son urged him on.

Disappointingly, both upper and lower gut endoscopies came out clean. I say 'disappointingly' because there comes a time when a grim diagnosis is better than no diagnosis. I have tussled with patients who express profound frustration at negative laboratory results—I always ask them if they would have been happier to get a laboratory return showing cancer.

From experience, most would prefer a definitive diagnosis to a string of negative results. Closure and certainty are a balm to the soul.

I faced the family and expressed my regrets about the results, while assuring them that this was a journey and that every negative result was at least a step closer to the final destination. By then, we were facing a twin crisis. During this one admission, he had been transfused six pints of blood, a rare feat in a hospital used to having dry blood banks.

On the one hand, I worried about iron overload from the multiple transfusions he had received, about twenty-two in less than six months. But I was more worried about the rate at which his haemoglobin was plummeting. After stopping the transfusion, we noticed a precipitous fall in haemoglobin, from eight to five, in less than five days. We needed to act fast and decisively.

I was on the phone with haematologists and gastroenterologists, who went through routine questioning of what I had done. The haematologist thought we needed more testing to rule out a marrow disorder called pure red cell aplasia. The gastroenterologist thought we needed a capsule endoscopy to rule out a small intestinal bleed. I reasoned that if he had a bleed that caused such a fall in blood, surely the bleeding should be apparent.

I decided to go with the haematologist's suggestion. We performed a cytogenetic analysis of the bone marrow specimen already extracted earlier. Further, I ordered tests for autoimmune markers and parvovirus B19, a virus closely associated with red cell aplasia. I sent him for a CT bleed scan, which images the blood vessels and may identify a leaky artery. It was negative.

I was already working in crisis mode because these tests would take time, and I was not sure what would happen during the intervening period.

Already itching to go home, I started him on a course of steroids, a kind of last-ditch effort to treat what I thought might be the problem—a sort of roll of the dice in darkness.

His blood counts kept coming down as we awaited the tests, necessitating another admission for transfusion. The steroids were not working. His sugars were creeping up, seemingly opening another front in an indeterminate war.

When the test results were emailed to me, I opened them trembling, hoping for an illumination of what was happening to Geoffrey. I was disappointed.

I called the son and, in a circuitous manner, explained to him that the diagnosis remained elusive. He expressed frustration. They seemed to have had enough.

"I suggest I refer you to another colleague or hospital for another evaluation." I offered, explaining that I thought that going to a hospital would be worse because it meant being handled by different hands who would not be patient enough to follow the story from where it started. We agreed he would see another specialist in Nairobi, a haemato-oncologist. I wrote them a detailed report on the steps we had taken so far.

The evaluation in Nairobi proved futile as the consultant insisted on another round of endoscopy. Geoffrey would have none of this. He phoned me from Nairobi and requested I continue treating him even if it meant he was dying in my hands.

We are often taught as doctors that learning in medicine never ends. You meet a case that sends you back to books.

I found myself poring over haematology and gastroenterology books, mining and sifting through information on anaemia. I hoped to land a clue in some text or research paper that would serve as my eureka moment in this case. None appeared to materialise.

By the time he had forty transfusions, he was exhausted mentally, physically, and financially. He had been admitted every week, always on the brink of collapse from critical anaemia. No sooner had his blood been replenished than it would come crashing again.

He held a fundraising campaign for a capsule endoscopy, which I had mentioned to them would be our next, if not last, frontier.

I heard his relatives mention going to India for an opinion, but they backed off whenever I took them through the merits and demerits of that move.

I turned to a general surgeon to hear their opinion.

"I know diagnostic laparotomies are an archaic way of making a diagnosis. Could you be willing to open an abdomen to search for the cause of anaemia?"

He looked a little perplexed. Whereas we thought the source of the bleeding was the small intestines, we both wondered how a surgeon would evaluate the more than six metres of tortuous gut to get a source of bleeding. Worse still, the bleeder could be in the lumen!

Then I dropped a bombshell.

"What about complete resection of the small intestines?" It is better for someone to live without the small gut than die with it intact.

The surgeon looked even more befuddled. Besides the enormous risk the procedure posed, there was no certainty that the bleeding was in the small gut, if there was any at all.

And that's where my attempt to engage the surgeon ended, as we hoped that a capsule endoscopy would be performed soon.

It was not to be.

A day after the last discharge, the wife found him collapsed in bed, gasping for breath. She let out a scream, attracting the attention of the farmhand. They rushed him to the nearest health centre. There was no pulse. After a few attempts at cardiopulmonary resuscitation, the two nurses pronounced him dead. He was paper-white, a testimony to a sudden drop in his haemoglobin.

I was heartbroken and discouraged. I mentioned to the son the need for an autopsy, but the family would hear none of it. For eight months, they had passed through the jungle of medicine and emerged bruised. Not only had they exhausted their savings, but they had also sold property in their pursuit of an elusive diagnosis.

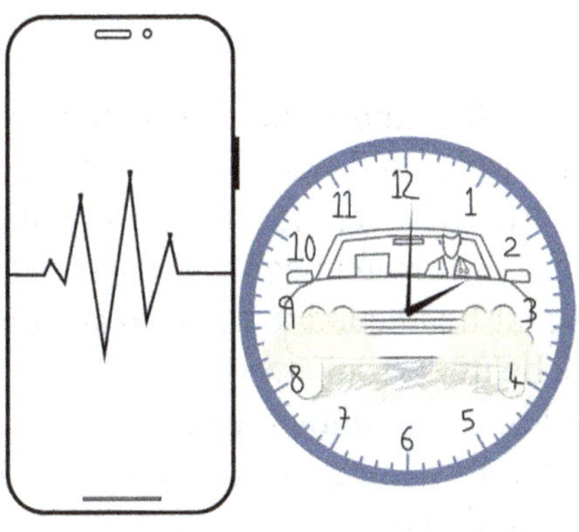

CHAPTER 3

A PHYSICIAN'S NIGHT CALLS

I HAD FORMED A HABIT of muting my phone at night. Even when your phone is muted, sometimes out of intuition or unexplained phenomena, you reach for it just in time for an important call.

I don't know what prompted my sudden loss of sleep, but I woke up to continuous blinking from my phone one Monday morning. When I looked at the list of missed calls, I was terrified that someone was dead, and I had slept through it. I was shocked.

Meru County Governor Kiraitu Murungi enjoyed robust health until COVID-19 struck. One Thursday afternoon, he called me to his office and confided in me that he felt fatigued and suspected he might have COVID-19. I checked his temperature. I auscultated his chest. All seemed normal. A nasopharyngeal swab he had taken returned negative. I assured him all was well and that he needed to take a rest from the gruelling work he undertook every day.

I called him the following day, Friday, after he had a series of rallies and project inspections. He sounded tired and told me that he was merely surviving. I asked him to take total rest for the weekend, but he was adamant that he had an important event on Saturday, after which he would take a short leave.

The next thing I saw was an alarming post by a prominent Kenyan blogger on Twitter, now X, after billionaire Elon Musk acquired it. It was short and tacit.

'Governor Kiraitu Meru ...'

It did not elaborate further, but the flurry of responses underneath the tweet was alarming. Most of the responders seemed to conclude that he was dead. I remembered the assurances I had given him and felt a twinge of fear and guilt cut through my chest.

I called him frantically to no avail. I left him a message that I needed to know how he was doing and that I had seen some mention of his health on social media.

"Good evening, Dr Karau. I'm admitted with COVID-19 at Nairobi Hospital. All is well. I will call you."

The message calmed my nerves but still brought a sense of inadequacy on my part—having seen him, I should have ordered more tests, perhaps a scan of the chest, to further rule out the diagnosis. But alas, no test is one hundred per cent sensitive.

Throughout his hospitalisation, I followed up on his progress through my colleagues at Nairobi Hospital. Whenever I could not reach him, I called his wife.

The governor, ever the philosopher, penned a moving piece in the *Sunday Nation* on 25 April 2021. He recounted his heroic battle with the virus, how he had returned several negative tests despite the fevers, extreme fatigue, confusion and sore throat, and how a final CT scan of the chest and a fourth COVID test came positive. This article highlighted his personal battle with the possibility of death, coming at a time when Tanzanian President John Pombe Magufuli had died. He drew powerful lessons on friendship, family, health, and peace of mind from his battle.

I visited him several times during his prolonged recovery, and our bond grew stronger. I became a close advisor on his health; he could call me whenever he felt unwell. He recovered and resumed the frenetic pace of work at Meru County until one Sunday morning when he called me.

"*Daktari,* I feel tired and feverish. Could you check on me?"

I was preparing to go to church. I asked my wife to accompany me to his Nkũbũ home.

I found him jovial, and he seemed to be in good health. We talked about other things until I interrupted him and told him I needed to examine him. We went to a separate room.

He seemed optimistic that he wasn't very bad, but his wife sounded more alarmed. She cautioned that he might run out of breath after a few steps. His breathing was growing more laboured. I percussed and auscultated his chest and felt crepitations on the lower aspect of the left lung, a sign of pneumonia.

I explained to them that he possibly had pneumonia, but the COVID diagnosis earlier in the year might have left some damage in the lungs. We needed to undertake some blood tests to see the extent of inflammation in the lungs and, if needed, a chest radiograph or a CT scan.

"We will do anything you tell us," he declared.

I summoned a laboratory technologist from Meru to draw blood samples for a wide range of tests. I advised him to take paracetamol as we awaited the tests.

In the evening, I was back at his home. Ever the worker, he had left home late in the afternoon to check on a Mr Ndubi, his primary school teacher. We reviewed the tests and concluded that he needed antibiotics. Thanks to his assistant, the drugs were bought that evening.

Everything appeared perfect when we left his home at 11:00 PM. He escorted us to our car, and I reminded his wife to call me if she sensed things were not going well.

Since becoming a consultant physician, I have kept my phone on overnight, always ready to help whenever called upon. Most of the calls would come from Meru Teaching and Referral Hospital. In most cases, I would advise my juniors on what to do until I report to work in the morning. A few cases would require me to drive to the hospital, which I always did.

However, as my practice grew and many people accessed my private number, I started receiving what I regarded as annoying calls in the middle of the night. A call would come through at 2:00 AM, and a seemingly drunk voice would ask, "Hallo. What drug can I take after getting too drunk?"

Another time:

"I'm feeling pain in my neck after sleeping on my pillow. What can I do?"

Yet another one: "Will you be available in your clinic next week?"

A person would find it fit to ask about my availability in a week's time, in the dead of the night. Some callers asked what they would take after alcohol-induced vomiting, chewing too much miraa and other concerns.

I initially responded to these questions until I became bothered by this trend, which disturbed my sleep pattern. I, therefore, formed a habit of muting my phone for the night unless I was on hospital call.

I left the governor's residence, muted my phone and went to sleep until early the following morning when I woke up to a flurry of calls.

I looked at the list of missed calls: ten from the governor's wife, over ten from the county minister for health, and a further five from the governor's personal assistant. There were numerous calls from Dr Saoli, a medical officer at Meru Teaching and Referral Hospital.

Terrified, I woke my wife and told her I feared the governor might have died. We reasoned how to go about this—who to call and how I would explain that I was unreachable on the phone when I was most needed.

I called Dr Saoli. She recounted that Governor Kiraitu had come to the hospital at 2:00 AM, feverish and shaking. She had trouble deciding on the next best step, no wonder, struck by the enormity of caring for the county chief.

It was the best of coincidence for Dr Saoli. She was one of our best students in the second medical class at Kenya Methodist University. On the day we had a finalists' dinner at Three Steers Hotel in Meru, the governor was holding a meeting there. We asked him to stop by and greet the newly graduated doctors.

During his short speech, he asked them if they would want to work in Meru County. The graduating doctors had already chosen their hospital stations for internship and had been posted accordingly.

Posting for medical officer interns is done through balloting. It happened that earlier in the day, during the balloting for the available internship stations in the country, only Dr Saoli was selected to undertake her internship at Meru Teaching and Referral Hospital. She protested furiously because, like all interns, she felt she needed the experience of another hospital, having already trained at Meru Teaching and Referral Hospital, which serves as the teaching hospital for Kenya Methodist University. However, the national government, which is responsible for posting medical officer interns, would not change her posting.

So, when the governor expressed his happiness that at least one newly graduated doctor had 'chosen' to work in Meru, he pointed at me and asked that I take her to his office. I eventually took her to the governor's office when she had finished her internship. During the next county hiring of doctors on permanent terms, she was picked.

Having personally met the governor in his office and having secured employment in Meru County, Dr Saoli was no stranger to the governor. Treating him was a strange twist of coincidence, and it was overwhelming, if not intimidating, for her.

We reasoned with my wife that if an unfavourable outcome had befallen the governor in my sleep, the best person to call was Dr Saoli.

"The governor came three hours ago, feverish and having chills. He appears stable, and we are preparing to transfer him to Nairobi." She informed me.

My relief was palpable and deep.

"Here, you can speak to him." She handed the phone to him.

Sounding groggy, he assured me that he was not very sick, only that people around him were panicking for no good reason. I attempted to apologise for not picking up the many calls, but he brushed it off, saying he knew I was exhausted by the demands of my work.

Next, I called his wife, who comforted me and reassured me that she perfectly understood why I slept with my phone on silent mode. I assured them that I would make calls to Nairobi Hospital to prepare for his prompt admission upon arrival.

I called Dr Frank Mwongera and Dr Irimu, and they began preparing for the governor's arrival at Nairobi Hospital.

Throughout the journey, I kept calling the first lady.

The governor was admitted with pneumonia, as I had diagnosed. The oral drugs had not started working by the time he was taken ill that night. This second admission did not take long before he was discharged. It, however, did not prevent the rumour mills from speculating about his death.

I saw him at his home, sometimes on domiciliary oxygen, but always stoic and reassuring. Within weeks, he was back on his feet and back in the office.

To this day, I have not solved the dilemma of whether to sleep with my phone silent, switched off, or on.

Such is the daily struggle that physicians must live with.

CHAPTER 4

SO LONG A JOURNEY

IN THE FACE OF CHRONIC diseases, the physician is not only a healer. They must learn to take the role of an escort, shepherding the patient through the tumultuous and perilous journey of life. They at once become a comforter, a source of encouragement, and a shoulder to lean on.

Jane was 24 years old when she started noticing the gradual loss of her hair. Her hairline kept receding, and oftentimes, she would wake up with tufts of hair having fallen from her scalp. She also noticed generalised lassitude creeping in. She felt weak and fatigued at slight exertion.

The journey through sickness usually begins with optimism. Even when evidence is overwhelming that something major is happening in the body, the patient will wait for improvement. They hope that a new day will come with healing. They are comfortable putting off a doctor's visit until it is no longer feasible.

"I noticed mouth sores, which came and went," she told me when I first saw her.

Her joints ached, and she quickly attributed it to the low temperatures where she worked. She had even made attempts to be transferred to a low-altitude area. She is a teacher.

By the time I saw her, she had seen a number of clinicians and doctors. She had been treated for arthritis. At one point, she presented with fevers and was medicated on antimalarials.

Yet when I saw her, all her manifestations appeared to fit a jigsaw puzzle. She had systemic lupus erythematosus (SLE).

Lupus is an autoimmune disease that affects almost all organs in the body. Antibodies are misdirected at body organs, ravaging the skin, joints, internal organs like lungs, kidneys and the brain.

"This is most probably lupus," I told her.

"But we need a battery of tests to confirm the diagnosis," I added as she looked at me, unbothered by what I thought was a bombshell.

The enormity of the diagnosis was not apparent to Jane. Sometimes it is the doctor who must bear the burden of grieving a difficult diagnosis because the patient is shielded from it by inadequate knowledge.

"Doc, I hope the problem will be cured quickly now that it is known," she asserted rather optimistically.

"Let's discuss this at length once the tests are out."

I utilised the one-week interlude as we awaited her tests to refresh my knowledge of this multisystem disease. I specifically concentrated on what advice I would offer her, what referrals I would make, and how I would put it to her in a simple yet reassuring manner.

The antinuclear antibody titres came back sky-high, as did the anti-double-strand DNA levels—two tests that form the backbone of the lupus diagnosis.

I ushered her into my office. As calmly as possible, I explained what lupus is, how it affects the body, and the potential dangers associated with it.

"The biggest problem with lupus is nephritis, which happens when the antibodies destroy kidney tissue and cause kidney failure," I told her.

However, I reassured her that the goal of treatment would be to forestall such an occurrence and minimise the risk of flare-ups.

"For how long are we going to do this, Daktari?"

Discussing the length of treatment of chronic disease is a touchpoint for many patients. A lifelong diagnosis is like a life sentence in jail. It is not easy to tell a 24-year-old that she will be on medications for the rest of her life. It comes out as measuring her life and numbering it in days and weeks.

"Well, this is a chronic disease. You will need lifelong follow-up and medications. But from the evidence, it is manageable."

Her mood darkened, and she became tense and gloomy.

"Jane, this is a journey. We need to walk the journey together. I will be referring you to specialists once in a while, but I'm ready to act as the escort in this journey." I told her.

"Promise you won't leave me," she sounded worried.

"I promise," I assured her.

The first part of the journey involved starting on medications and dealing with the adverse effects.

I came to cherish Jane's optimism and drive in life. She dealt with the drugs calmly and did not blame doctors easily, as it happens when drugs cause nausea or diarrhoea. She handled the multiple admissions stoically; every time I saw her, she would be confident of complete healing.

"You know, Doc, this disease might not be curable, but it is healable, and I know that healing comes from God."

She made me understand the difference between cure and healing. Whereas many chronic diseases have means of control or management but no cure, healing comes from making peace with the diagnosis and believing in a higher purpose than oneself.

Yet the journey of lupus is fraught with difficulties and surprises.

I got a call from Jane's fiancé that she had difficulty breathing one night. I advised him to take her to St Theresa Kiirua Mission Hospital, where I would review her early in the morning.

I found her in respiratory distress, an oxygen mask supplying a gush of air and covering most of her face. She had sustained a pulmonary embolism. The anticoagulation medication took effect quickly, and she was on her way to full recovery in three days. But more surprises lay ahead.

At 26, she was already jittery that she was taking too long to conceive. The fiancé was already showing signs of fatigue with her frequent admissions and the many drugs she took. She was always tired and in pain. She would be in remission only to suffer a flare-up with no identifiable aggravating factor.

She was seen by an obstetrician-gynaecologist who recommended ovulation-inducing tablets. Two months later, she missed her periods. A home-test kit came positive for pregnancy. She felt uplifted.

The next time I saw her, she was admitted with torrential vaginal bleeding. She had lost the pregnancy.

We went back to the drawing board and worked her up for antiphospholipid syndrome, a rare subset of lupus. It was positive. It explained the pulmonary embolism and the pregnancy loss. This only meant that the number of tablets she took daily increased as we added anticoagulants and antiplatelet medications.

You can have everything figured out in a journey, but you must leave room for surprises. The unexpected can happen and force you to turn back, change course or even spend the night on the road. What you must never compromise is your drive and the hope that you will reach the destination.

As with many other patients, the journey with Jane reminded me of an anecdote I had heard: Two young fish swim in a pond, enjoying the early morning sun. They happen to meet an older fish swimming in the opposite direction.

"Young boys, how is the water this morning?" the older fish asks.

"Very well," they reply in unison, passing each other.

The two young fish swim on for a while until one looks at the other in bewilderment and asks, "By the way, what the hell is water?"

The story illustrates how we ignore the obvious as we aim for the destination.

Therefore, it is imperative that in life's journey, enjoying the little detours and the small joys of every day is as important as focusing on the destination.

One day, I asked Jane how she was coping, and she told me that she was focused on gratitude for each day and where she had reached.

By the time she was celebrating her twenty-eighth birthday, her fiancé had left her. He started by giving excuses that his family was against their relationship. He quietly left the house they shared. He started ignoring her calls and text messages and slowly but surely vanished from her life, leaving her heartbroken and empty.

"I think he was not ready to walk the journey with me, seeing how difficult it has become," Jane told me on one of the visits when I asked her why she had come alone.

I also noticed that she walked with a limp, which she told me was because of a nagging pain in her left hip. I didn't think much about it until I saw her two weeks later. I was alarmed because we had agreed on a review in two months.

"The pain in my left groin is worsening."

I couldn't wrap my head around what was happening. I ordered a pelvic x-ray. The results were disheartening: Both her femoral heads were shrunken and diminished, a clear case of *avascular necrosis*. This means that the blood supply to the knob-shaped head of the thigh bone is cut short, and the bone dies out.

I phoned the rheumatologist, who agreed that lupus could cause this, though it is rare. Steroids, one of the drugs she was on, could also cause this.

"This will need total hip replacement," I told her as I wrote a note to the orthopaedic surgeon.

To have prosthetic hip joints on both sides at the age of 28 years is unfathomable, but for Jane, there was going to be no other option. She categorically refused the surgery, and after a conference with the rheumatologist, the orthopaedic surgeon and Jane, we agreed to watch and wait.

It took six months to convince her, or, to put it more accurately, for her to be convinced.

She became dependent on crutches to walk, and would need help to stand from a seated position. The pain became excruciating, and she needed tramadol and other opioids every few hours to maintain her sanity.

When she finally agreed to see the orthopaedic surgeon to plan for bilateral total hip replacement, she did so with grace and courage.

"We shall replace the head of the femur with a prosthetic joint. I suggest starting with the left hip because it appears more damaged." The surgeon counselled her.

"Go ahead, Doc. I'm ready for anything," she nonchalantly replied.

I took over her care after the procedure. My work as a physician was to ensure she did not contract infection, did not suffer clotting of blood in her veins (for which she was highly predisposed) and that her liver, kidneys and heart were properly monitored.

She took everything in her stride, always courageous and calm, as if impervious to pain and worry, a worry that pervaded my body. Pain control was initially adequate until the anaesthetic medications wore off. She began wincing, grimacing and eventually crying in pain. To her collection of anticoagulants, immunomodulatory, antibiotic and analgesic medications, I added opioid analgesics.

When dealing with many drugs, the challenge is to ensure they don't react with each other, augment certain adverse effects, or even cancel out the benefits of each other. It is more like a game of chess where every move matters, and one indecisive move can put you into a cul-de-sac and spoil the entire game.

The human body is complicated. It can spring surprises. Often, physicians may not know what will spring up until they are confronted with a condition that sends them on a spin.

On the third day post-operatively, Jane's blood pressure surged. When the nurse called me, I attributed it to pain and anxiety. I initially tried *verbocain,* slang for encouragement and counselling, to calm her down. Instead, the numbers increased worryingly, and we feared a stroke. This new battlefront required the determination and authority of a commander, as well as the passion of a foot soldier. We combined two drugs, but the blood pressure kept surging. By the time we achieved some semblance of control, we were on five different anti-hypertensive medications, each at supranormal doses.

At discharge, the orthopaedic surgeon advised that she use crutches and avoid weight-bearing on the left hip for at least two weeks.

It is common for patients to leave the most critical aspects of their care to their physicians. I see this commonly in chronic disease patients battling hypertension, diabetes, heart failure, stroke, and neuropathies. Even among the educated, few will take the pains to know what drugs they are using. Most don't know their diagnoses and will not care or remember to ask.

A gentleman on eight drugs will enter the consultation room without any clue about his medications, recent investigations, and scans.

"Which drugs are you currently taking?" I often ask patients.

"I can't properly remember, but there is a red tablet, a pink tablet, and one that has the colour of your desk." To which I always retort, inwardly, that my training is not about mastering the colours of tablets!

Now, on fifteen different drugs, Jane came for her mandatory two-week review. I was impressed by her recovery. She could now bear little weight on her left hip. Her face was bright and relaxed. But more assuredly, she knew all her drugs, their dosages and timings.

Save for slight oedema of the ankles occasioned by nifedipine, a blood pressure medication, she seemed to be holding out well against this multi-pronged enemy who threatened to overwhelm her defences.

In our medical centre, where I saw day patients, the nurse would bring files for me to review briefly before patients arrived. Over 80% of the time, I felt a little anxious, even jittery, about facing patients. Some would complain of the most mundane of symptoms, while others, who had evidently improved, would curse the way treatment was taking a toll on them. In such cases, my work shifts from pure physician work, which deals with organisms, faulty systems, and perturbed physiology, to attempting to rewire the brain to adopt a more positive view of life.

With Jane, every review was a pleasure—she carried herself with grace and stoicism, and you would have to dig deep into her file and ask questions to get a hint of the slightest regret.

She underwent a successful hip replacement and now walks with a spring in her gait. The nagging pain that opened the floodgates of surgery has disappeared. She faces each day at a time, secure in the knowledge that each day is different and that each day comes with its blessings, pains, burdens and pleasures.

I continue to walk the journey with Jane. That's my calling.

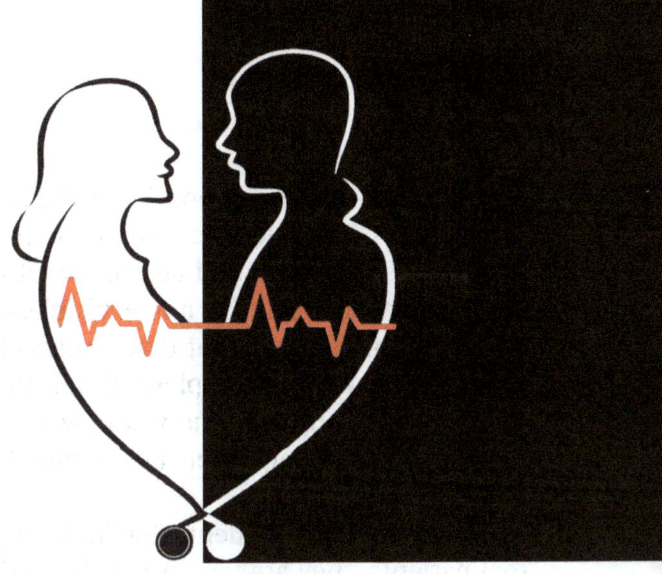

CHAPTER 5

MAN, WITHOUT WOMAN, IS NOTHING

FOR MANY CENTURIES, MEDICINE HAS been taught in a similar fashion. Medical students are first introduced to the basic sciences. Human anatomy, medical physiology, and medical biochemistry form the cornerstones of training. They then proceed to other preclinical sciences that form the subsequent blocks of the foundation—microbiology, haematology, pathology and clinical chemistry.

Through the two or three years they are learning these foundational courses, it is not uncommon to hear some of them complain or mumble in exasperation that this is not the medicine they came to study. It is analogous to a tall building; the foundation must run deep and be reinforced with strong metal and concrete. It will not be visible. I have heard some contractors comment that owners of these skyscrapers sometimes complain about these 'buried millions'. But, anyway, who would want to see their multi-story building come down tumbling after a storm?

Before medical students begin interacting with real patients, they are taught the theoretical aspects of history-taking. Yes, the thrust of medicine, even in this epoch of technology, rests on what the patient tells you.

A proper history will consist of the patient's biodata, major complaints (and how long they have been experienced). The next portion consists of an elucidation of the history of the presenting illness. Thus, a patient who says they have had pain in the foot for ten years will explain why they chose to seek care on this particular day. They will be probed to explain the character of the pain, the intensity, and if it radiates or spreads elsewhere. They will be required to explain if they have noticed any manoeuvres or practices that aggravate or mitigate the pain. Sometimes, an impatient patient will wonder what all these questions aim to achieve. But medical teachers insist they must be asked, with military precision, without fail. They form the basis of reasoning towards a diagnosis.

Once all the symptoms have been exhausted, the student must learn to take a social history. It entails asking the patient where they come from, if they are married, what they do for a living, if they take alcohol or smoke cigarettes, if they have many sexual partners, *et cetera*.

A careful teacher will realise that most students breeze through family and social history without giving it careful thought. Medicine has always prided itself on being a logical and scientific profession—no procedure or step is taken for the sake of it. It must be calculated with the patient's best interest in mind.

I always get my interns laughing whenever I ask them if the male patient is married. Through keen observation, you will notice that certain male patients are dishevelled, unkempt, drooling, hopeless and sincerely lost in the labyrinth of the disease. They seem to have long given up the fight, even as medics struggle.

The male ward in many public hospitals in the global south is a spectacle of desperation and suffering. Men do not just seek care until the pain is unbearable, they can't breathe properly, or they are on the verge of dying.

But not all men.

In the adjacent female wards, you will find well-kempt and hopeful ladies, notwithstanding their grim diagnoses.

When daughters visit their mothers or aunts, they change their clothes, clean them again after nurses have cleaned them, apply oil on their faces, and have them lie well.

For the few married men in our medical ward, their wives show up regularly, clean and feed them, change their clothes, and infuse life into them. The same happens to boys when their mothers visit them.

Studies have shown that married men live better and longer. The magnitude of marital protection appears to be greater for younger than older patients, but old unmarried men have the worst suffering I have ever seen. It is one thing to suffer infirmity, but a different, if not catastrophic, thing to suffer infirmity compounded by loneliness and destitution. This does not apply to widowed men who have an existing family structure.

Thus, whenever confronted by men in a pathetic state, I always want to know their marital and family status.

Woe unto the 40, 50 or 60-year-olds without wives. As the disease takes a toll on their body, devastation visits them like a hurricane, and their coarse beards and long hair advertise their suffering.

Indeed, from my anecdotal research, the single most determinant of death in a medical ward is whether the man is married or not.

Mostly, these men are drunkards who threw away their wives or a few who chose not to marry because of their misery, and instead of joining a monastery, they still live as normal men.

Unmarried men must maintain connections with siblings or relatives who can take care of them. Disease can strike like a thief when least expected and least prepared for. And even when relatives are available, you will see women relatives taking the role of caregivers with dedication and love.

We underestimate the role of women in our lives, but we must realise that they actually keep the heart pumping.

Whereas men indulge in 'big things' like buying cars, land, paying fees and all that, ladies do what keeps life moving: They clean after us, organise the house, feed us and ensure we sleep soundly.

These roles are more important when life is threatened. When malaria takes you down, your car doesn't come to your rescue. The woman in your life ensures you are fed, and your feverish forehead is dabbed with cold water.

This does not in any way deprecate the place of women in a constantly evolving society. Rather, it points to their maternal instincts, which swing into action when their own are threatened. It is a phenomenon observed not only in humans but also in many mammalian species. The female lion will risk her life to hunt for her cubs, even as the males rest their hefty manes while sleeping away. Their primary role is to fight, expand their territories, and demonstrate their power. But they will be among the first in the feeding frenzy when the female brings down an eland.

Social history in the medical context is, therefore, not a mechanistic requirement for medical students, nurses, and doctors; rather, it is an important cog in the proper care of the patient. It prepares the medical team to know what to do and what to expect.

In medicine, women play a critical role as the real engine where life begins and moves.

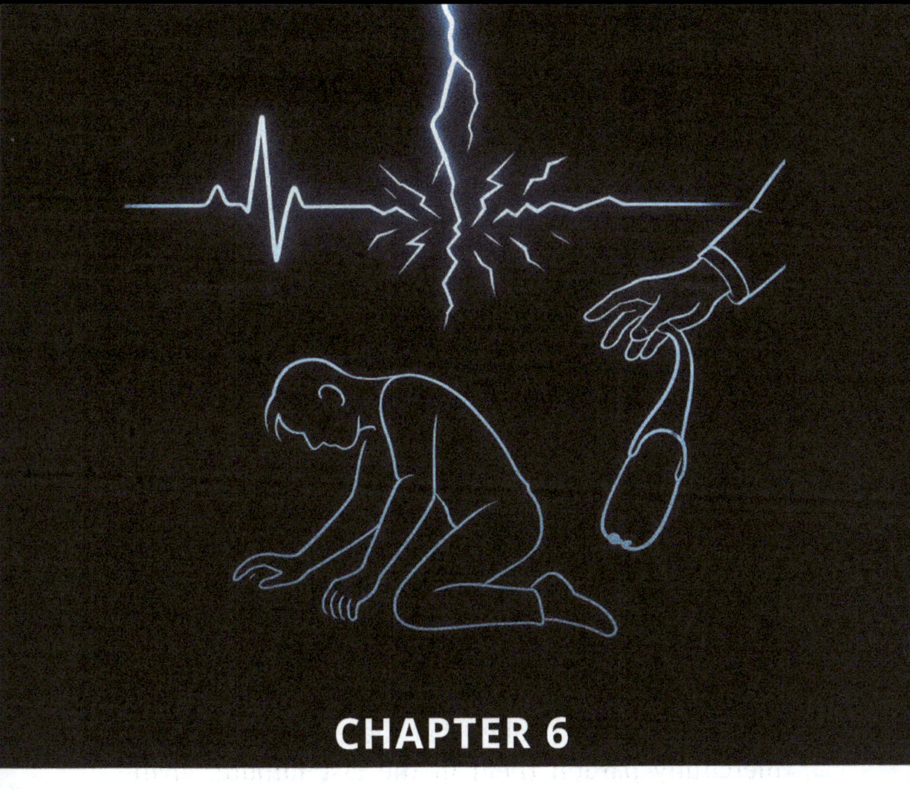

CHAPTER 6

WHEN DEATH COMES OUT OF THE BLUE

AS A DOCTOR, DEATH IS never far away from you. Almost every day, you are a solemn witness to the terminal cycle of life. It comes with a certain level of denial, even for the experienced physician. You meet a patient with metastatic liver disease who has lapsed into hepatic encephalopathy. You stand guard as his brain function deteriorates despite your frantic efforts. You see death approaching, but somehow, you feel that something small, a bit more, can be done, and the patient miraculously wakes up. Deep within, you know that this is a lost battle, but you harbour *delusions of reprieve.*

Famously postulated by Dr Viktor Frankl, the famous Austrian neurologist-psychiatrist who survived the Nazi concentration camps, delusions of reprieve represent the last hope for a condemned prisoner.

Viktor Frankl was an unfortunate witness and survivor of the Nazi death machine. He watched, haplessly, as prisoners were randomly picked up and sent to the firing squad or gas chambers.

Those condemned to die would, until the last minute, have a strong belief that the executioner would mercifully pardon them in the last minute, giving them a fresh lease of life. It seldom happened.

Doctors taking care of dying patients somehow suffer from these delusions, even as they prepare for the inevitable. But what happens when death comes out of the blue to a seemingly stable patient while in the middle of a safe procedure?

When this quagmire hit me like a thunderbolt, I was a freshly qualified internist. At the teaching hospital where I worked, I would conduct ward rounds in the company of final-year undergraduate medical students. They presented patients they had clerked before the ward round.

It typically proceeds as follows: the student provides a comprehensive patient history and examination and outlines the diagnostic formulation. The house intern takes over and then brings the reality of what is happening. I would then summarise by asking more questions, confirming some examination findings, reviewing the file to examine the tests, scans, and drug chart, and finally making recommendations on the way forward. This formula served the dual purpose of teaching future doctors while managing the patient.

On this sunny Wednesday morning, I finished the rounds earlier than usual. Almost all patient cases were straightforward, most work-ups were performed, and the diagnosis was clinched. I felt elated and victorious in completing the usually arduous task without breaking much sweat.

I sauntered around the amenity ward and greeted the nurses at the nursing station. The head nurse requested that I do a bone marrow aspiration on a patient who was waiting on the benches outside the ward. The doctor who was supposed to do it had been caught up in an emergency, and the old lady had waited for a long time.

I looked at the file. She was a 68-year-old lady with no known comorbidities[1] who needed a bone marrow aspiration to evaluate her low platelet and red blood cell counts. Her examination, according to the notes, had yielded no clues. She was not on any medications that could cause this aberration. She had no swollen lymph nodes (lymph glands in the neck, armpits, or groin area). Her mouth was devoid of any gum

---

[1] The coexistence of two or more related medical conditions.

hypertrophy[2], bleeding or sores. Her abdomen was soft, with no enlargement of the spleen. A peripheral blood film had shown no firm leads.

A bone marrow aspiration is a simple bedside procedure that involves inserting a firm needle into the cavity between the layers of bone and aspirating the blood-like marrow for analysis. It is done under local anaesthesia, an injection around the site that numbs the skin and the *periosteum,* the outer layer of bone, which is usually quite sensitive to pain.

The main complications include prolonged pain, bleeding, introduction of an infection into the bone, and inadvertent internal injuries through the introduction of the needle to the lungs or the heart.

Her platelet count was 30, a safe level for such an invasive procedure.

I ushered her into the procedure room. She was a pleasant lady, clad in a flowing black *bui bui*. Her daughter, dressed in a similar outfit, accompanied her.

I explained the procedure to them, as the laboratory assistant marked glass slides and vacutainers to obtain and transport the bone marrow samples for further analysis.

Bone marrow aspiration can be done in the posterior iliac crest, the bony prominence above the buttocks, or the sternum, the central bone in the front of the chest. The former is preferred because there are

---

[2] Abnormal enlargement of a body part or organ.

no vital organs nearby, and the marrow yield is usually better.

As I exposed her right gluteal region, I palpated the abdomen to check one more time if the spleen was enlarged. It was not. I placed my stethoscope over her precordium[3]. The cardiac sounds were regular and of normal intensity.

I marked the site with a pen and cleaned it with iodine. I infiltrated the skin and the bone with lignocaine, a local anaesthesia. She gave me a thumbs-up when the pain ceased.

Using my right hand, as is procedure, I drilled the bone marrow needle into her iliac crest while stabilising it with my palm. The resistance gave way, signalling that I was in the marrow cavity within no time, thanks to osteoporosis, the softening of the bones that is prevalent in older women. I aspirated the marrow, and I saw her wince in pain as the marrow flowed into the syringe, a further confirmation that I was in the right place. I drew out the needle, handed the syringe to the lab assistant to prepare the slides, and put the rest in an anticoagulant-impregnated vacutainer.

The procedure took less than ten minutes, but the events that followed took two hours.

I looked at the patient to victoriously announce that we had completed the procedure. She was unresponsive. The nurse gave me a grave look. We knew something was amiss.

---

[3] The part of the body over the heart and lower chest.

I quickly checked the pulse. It was absent. Grace, the nurse, quickly summoned two other nurses from the nursing station. We mobilised a resuscitation tray and started performing cardiopulmonary resuscitation.

We gave a few shots of adrenaline as we compressed the chest and administered oxygen within intervals of the chest compressions. Fear gripped me, and I could feel my face turning ashen, the colour draining away as the enormity of the situation settled in. It didn't take us long to realise that we had lost the battle.

I have never felt as terrible in my life as I did that day. I don't believe in fate, but the events of that morning appeared preternatural. How I finished the rounds earlier than usual, strayed into the amenity ward, and agreed to lend a hand on a procedure that was not mine—it all seemed fateful, if not completely inexplicable.

Our worry was how to break the news of this cataclysmic event to the daughter, who sat on the bench outside, oblivious to the blow we had just suffered. As if driven by a hidden force, she knocked on the door and demanded to know if we had finished the procedure. The nurse calmly told her to wait outside.

She sensed the gravity of the situation when Grace called her into one of the empty nursing rooms within the amenity department.

"Tell me what's happening with Mum!" She demanded.

"Calm down; we shall let you know in a minute," Grace calmly reassured her.

As if on cue, she began pacing up and down the room, reciting words from the Koran. I could pick up phrases like *'Allahu Akbar'* and *'Alhamdulillah',* but her incantations rose into a frenzy.

She might have seen my face, which I think was ashen because my skin had taken on a pallor that was almost ghostly, drained of all warmth and colour.

Broaching bad news has never been my strength. I struggle with it despite years of experience. I feel the weight of the responsibility to communicate the loss in a way that is both honest and gentle. I understand that my words will forever change the lives of the people I tell that their loved one is gone.

During our community health experience in the fourth year of medical training, I was attached to an HIV Voluntary Testing and Counselling Centre in Ruiru Health Centre, Kiambu. It all seemed easy as the counsellors took patients through pre-testing counselling. They would then show them the HIV testing strips. If your test produced one strip, it meant that you were negative. If two strips appeared, you had tested positive for HIV. Patients took the bad news in different strides.

One couple entered the counselling room together. During the counselling, the woman had accused the husband of infidelity and declared she wanted to know if he had contracted the virus. When the test results came out, she tested positive, while her husband tested negative. She collapsed and fainted. I could barely stand the spectacle.

The department required students to perform the entire counselling-testing-counselling cycle on their own. One day, the counsellor was called for a meeting and left me to perform the exercise. Two ladies came for testing. I attempted to do counselling, but one of the ladies was in a hurry and demanded that I go ahead and perform the real thing.

After drawing their blood samples, I ushered them out to wait for 10 minutes before they came in for disclosure of the results and post-test counselling. I threw a glance at the tests. Both were positive. I did not know how to summon the courage to disclose to them. Instead, I closed the room and walked out. While far away, I called the counsellor and requested him to do the disclosures. Luckily, he was within the hospital compound.

In hospitals, when faced with a grim diagnosis, uncertainty or death, we usually call a family conference. The next of kin, say the wife or husband or close relative of the patient, may be accompanied by close family members. It depends on the level of trust within the family.

The scene is usually sombre, and it is not unusual to palpate the silence that engulfs the room before the conversation begins. Tradition demands that the most senior doctor in the room lead the conference. Everyone introduces themselves as one of the nurses takes notes. He will explain everything about the patient, including the difficulties, prognosis, and potential treatments. At this point, he will ask the family members to ask questions and demand clarifications. Other members of the medical team may also chip in where necessary.

If a death has occurred, it is not unusual for family members to break down as the senior doctor skirts around the topic. Often, he will avoid mentioning death. He meanders around the patient's journey until he finally remarks that despite the best efforts, the victim succumbed. Some family members may descend into a thick cloud of silence, while others wail, chant, and fall into a state of pandemonium. Ethical and humane practice allows relatives to vent in the best possible way. Where necessary, additional medical support is called to treat those who suffer shock.

In the nursing room within the amenity department, our silence and my ashen look may have alerted Amina, the distraught daughter, that her mother had died.

I asked Amina to sit down, creating a more intimate and respectful setting. I carefully chose my words, speaking slowly and deliberately as I explained what we had done and what had eventually happened.

"Unfortunately, Mum did not ..."

"Wait, did you just say Mum died?"

"I'm so sorry," I said, my voice heavy with emotion. "Despite our best efforts, we were unable to ..."

"Mum, who walked herself here and was as fit as a fiddle?"

Grace nodded in the affirmative. Amina collapsed into a heap. We picked her up, placed her on a couch and ensured her breathing was normal.

When she woke up, she was groggy, as if someone had just woken up from a nightmare. She appeared to have calmed down.

"So, what do we do next?" She asked.

"Please call another relative to support you," I told her. Grace handed her a glass of water.

I escaped the room and left the hospital, my mind full of unanswered questions. Once outside the gate, I called Grace and asked if the daughter of the deceased would agree to an autopsy. She categorically refused.

The following day, I was entering the outpatient department when someone called me. It was Amina.

"Daktari, don't worry about yesterday. The will of God prevailed," Amina said.

I was lost for words and only replied with a nod.

Perhaps the old lady had suffered a fatal ventricular arrhythmia[4] induced by the local anaesthetic. But how were we to know?

How can we predict this so that the next patient doesn't suffer the same fate?

A doctor can be likened to the 'man in the arena', a speech delivered by President Theodore Roosevelt in the Sorbonne, France, in 1910:

"The credit belongs to the man who is actually in the arena, whose face is marred by dust and sweat and blood; who strives valiantly; who errs, who comes short again and again, because there is no effort without error and shortcoming; but who does actually strive to do the deeds; who knows great enthusiasms, the great devotions; who spends himself in a worthy cause; who at best knows, in the end, the triumph of

---

[4] Abnormal heart rhythms originating in the heart's lower chambers (ventricles), causing a rapid, irregular heartbeat and potentially life-threatening conditions like cardiac arrest.

high achievement, and who at the worst, if he fails, at least fails while daring greatly, so that his place shall never be with those cold and timid souls who neither know victory nor defeat."

In the arena of medicine, death can come out of the blue. As it knocks down the victim, it may also knock down the doctor. The doctor's confidence, passion, self-belief and even energy may be knocked. Death is never far from a doctor. They must strive in the arena they have chosen.

That, is what matters.

CHAPTER 7

LIVING THROUGH A PANDEMIC

IN 1899, AN ECCENTRIC GOAN doctor arrived by ship to Mombasa, the historic coastal city in Kenya, and boarded the train to the emerging town of Nairobi. Dr Rosendo Ribeiro was a Goan-Portuguese surgeon and a Member of the Royal College of Surgeons (MRCS). He was a go-getter and was ready to venture into the untrodden path.

In the early 1900s, nobody would have placed a bet on a city erupting out of a swampy shanty called Enkare Nairobie. However, the decision by the British railway engineers to establish a depot for their supplies during the construction of the Mombasa–Uganda railway continued to attract people like bees to nectar.

Within five years of the depot, the former swamp had become a bustling, dusty scene of Asians, Europeans, Arabs, and Africans. Europeans occupied Victoria Street, today's Tom Mboya Street, where they traded their wares. The Indian Bazaar sprang up on the western end of Victoria Street and was characterised by overcrowding and plagued by disease. Soon, other groups followed, hoping to benefit from the foreigners who had pitched tents in this Maasai territory, which contained swamps, black cotton soil, rivers, and savannah bushlands.

The Somalis, in particular, liked meat and opened butcheries, much to the chagrin of Asians, who were predominantly vegetarian. Africans rented tin shacks on today's River Road, which at the time formed the outer edge of the fledgling settlement and provided a diverse array of services, including prostitution.

Within six months of his arrival in Nairobi, Dr Rosendo set up a private day surgery in the Indian Bazaar Street. His memoirs contain vivid descriptions of the maladies he handled, as well as the clash of cultures, civilisations, and beliefs that characterised medical practice in this nascent city.

Malaria was a common ailment among all tribes, he writes. Indeed, he is renowned for discovering an antimalarial drug, the patent for which he sold to an international pharmaceutical company.

Among the Indians, anaemia was common, no doubt a result of poor dietary habits and overcrowding.

'Despite the severe anaemia, they refuse liver injections and all my prescriptions', he writes.

The Wakamba suffered from Kala-azar, which caused their spleens and livers to enlarge, and they went to surgery with distended bellies. They had a cultural habit of filing their teeth, and their dental hygiene was pathetic.

He recounts a case of a Somali woman who was brought to his clinic from 30 miles away for a tooth extraction. On examination, he realised that she had severe vaginal haemorrhage from obstructed labour due to locked twins. He offered to treat this serious condition instead of the dental extraction, but her carers categorically refused, saying that culturally, delivery was only done by women, and a foreigner could not perform it.

'I followed up to inquire about the fate of the woman after two days.' I was told that she died. The husband and other relatives simply shrugged their shoulders and remarked that it was the 'will of Allah'.

Dr Rosendo served with dedication and witnessed with his eyes as the once-shanty outpost grew into a city. In 1902, he saw a few patients presenting with fevers and enlarged lymph nodes.

Doctors, then as now, were trained to connect the dots to diagnose diseases they had not encountered during their training. It is impossible for a doctor to encounter all the diseases in the world by the time they complete medical training. But a sound application of medical principles will lead to diagnoses of previously unseen conditions.

Dr Rosendo connected the pattern of disease he was seeing with the environment they came from—all were residents of the overcrowded Bazaar Street, which by then was not only teeming with humanity but had also been colonised by hordes of rats. He was dealing with an outbreak of bubonic plague. Ever since Biblical times, the bubonic plague has caused dreaded plagues that decimated entire populations. In Europe, the Black Death of the 1300s is said to have killed over 25 million people. In the Republic of Genoa, rats allegedly sneaking from ships arriving from the port of Marseille caused a horrendous plague outbreak in the city in 1656. It was the fiercest and most devastating blow to the vibrant republic, greatly affecting its prospects.

In Nairobi, Dr Rosendo pondered over the next steps. Managing a plague in an emerging city with poor sanitation and a clash of cultures would be no easy task. Nevertheless, as one of the few qualified healthcare workers in the town, he quickly drew a plan of action and convinced the city administration that unless it were enforced, the entire population would perish.

Caused by *Yersinia pestis (Y. pestis),* a bacterium found in rodents and their fleas, bubonic plague is transmitted from rodents, such as rats, by the bites of infected fleas. It causes characteristic swelling of lymph glands (called buboes). The pneumonic form of the disease may cause fulminant pneumonia with respiratory failure. Ominously, this respiratory form can spread from person to person through the air.

Over the centuries, humans have struggled to contain infections that have reservoirs in wild animals.

Dr Rosendo's prescription was as radical as it was practical—to burn down the Indian Bazaar. To raze down the bustling business street and perish the buildings and wares.

By the time his recommendation found favour with the colonial administration, over 70 people had died. The crisis was escalating. Eventually, the town administration ordered the evacuation of the shanty street, which was dutifully razed. It is a testimony to Dr Rosendo's dutifulness that his surgical practice was also decimated in the exercise.

In an era of medical stagnation and poor access, the prescription of one brave doctor saved an emerging city and, perhaps, an entire civilisation.

Dr Rosendo was himself an eccentric, though committed doctor. Apart from his busy surgery, he worked as the Portuguese Consul in Kenya and handled house calls around the estates of the rapidly burgeoning city. He conducted deliveries and performed minor surgical procedures, including the removal of jiggers and the dispensing of medications to patients from diverse cultural backgrounds.

To add to his mythical nature was his preferred mode of transport—a domesticated zebra, which he rode amidst a cloud of dust as he traversed Nairobi City during the course of his duties. The enduring image of a tall man with a cowboy hat and boots astride a zebra is the story of an emerging city and a man who saved it at its moment of greatest peril.

Today, Dr Ribeiro Parklands High School in Nairobi's Parklands estate stands as a testimony to Dr Rosendo's other side—philanthropy. He donated the land upon which the school was built and helped mobilise funds to construct the first buildings. He relocated to London, where he lived in his final days, and passed away peacefully in 1951. Some of his eye-opening accounts of the struggles in this boiling cauldron of cultures, beliefs and religions were serialised in the British Medical Journal in 1954.

The lessons from this outbreak would come to the fore almost 120 years later when COVID-19 hit Nairobi.

Disease modelling experts know that the next pandemic is never far away. The world will, from time to time, witness pandemics. Each comes with its own lessons. Humans can never be 100% effective, even with lessons from the dawn of time.

Experts have devised steps to monitor and manage the next pandemic, but this will always fall short. The model involves monitoring zoonoses, understanding the pathogen (the genetic sequences and pathogenetic mechanisms), developing vaccines, locking down populations when needed and preparing for rapid production of vaccines when needed. The strategy has worked to some extent for Ebola haemorrhagic fever.

But what happens when a mutated virus, with no existing vaccine, causes strange symptomatology to arise? The most baffling human reaction is to ignore an occurrence in a faraway land and dismiss it as if it will not bother them.

When Coronavirus Disease of 2019 (COVID-19) was first detected in Wuhan, China, it seemed far away. Even to physicians like me, it seemed we were far removed from the happenings half a world away. We should have known better. Respiratory viruses tend to spread faster, especially in a globalised world.

Coronaviruses have been around for some time and have caused epidemics through their mutated variants. I recall when COVID-19 became a global issue, long before it reached the shores of Kenya. I dusted off my virology books and reminded myself of the biology of these organisms and the diseases they cause.

As stories began to emerge of mass mortalities from COVID-19 in Italy, China, and India, governments started taking notice. The World Health Organisation (WHO) issued guidelines on quarantining symptomatic or suspected individuals and cessation of travel from affected areas. Initially sceptical of the impact of the virus, the Chinese government imposed a total lockdown on the population of Wuhan.

In Kenya, the first case was reported by the Health Cabinet Secretary on 13 March 2020. The smiling young lady would become the poster child of the new disease that had finally reached the shores of Kenya and East Africa.

The initial response was to force the quarantine of affected individuals and their contacts. It was not going to be an easy exercise, as within a few days of quarantine, photos emerged of exasperated young patients breaking away from a quarantine facility and jumping over a fence.

Apart from tracking and testing contacts of COVID-19 victims, the government imposed a strict mask-wearing policy in public places and banned handshakes.

On 6 April 2020, the president announced a three-week lockdown in Nairobi, banning travel into and out of the city. A few hours before the lockdown came into effect, the city's roads were clogged with heavy traffic as people staged a mass exodus into the rural areas. Whether the lockdown was effective or not remains to be seen, as COVID-19 cases continued to rise and mortalities soared.

Our hospital held strategy meetings to develop a comprehensive plan for combating the virus. Some healthcare workers suggested closing the hospital, but the majority insisted that closing it during a pandemic was akin to closing the barracks in wartime. We would fight.

My first case of COVID-19 was the wife of a close friend. She presented with fevers and joint pains and would experience sweating at night. She visited a local dispensary, where she was given malaria tablets. A few days later, she noticed a diminishing sense of smell and a lingering cough. I listened to her intently and then carefully examined her chest, auscultating the area below the scapula. I picked fine crepitations. I informed her that I suspected she had COVID-19.

"*Daktari,* don't accuse me falsely," she told me, evidently angered by my suggestion.

"This is just an impression I have formed. The tests will prove us right or wrong. But you need not worry."

Her pulse oximetry showed oxygen levels at 86%, an eerily low saturation in blood. I calmly informed her that we did not have the luxury of time.

Only when she was confirmed the following day did I realise that I had worn no protection, including a face mask, during my encounter with her. I waited with bated breath for the emergence of symptoms, but none seemed to appear.

Over the course of the next few days, I developed my own algorithm for suspecting COVID-19.

Fever and body aches? Most likely.

Treated for malaria? Most likely.

Cough or sore throat? Most likely.

Diminished sense of smell? Most likely, although many patients were not quick to notice this symptom.

I would categorise patients for testing based on this simple classification. Over 90% of the time, my suspicion was proven right.

Within two months, the country and, indeed, the entire world were in a state of panic, as schools closed, flights were grounded, cities were locked down, and livelihoods were lost.

The government of Kenya spoke one language in enforcing the curfews and lockdowns, but police officers interpreted it with brutal gusto, clobbering stranded drivers and throwing them into cells.

"This disease is not a joke. If we treat it normally, it will treat us abnormally." This famous statement was attributed to the Kenya Health Cabinet Secretary, Mutahi Kagwe. His rallying call, "If you don't get it, it will get you", became the subject of jokes and comedy during these heady days.

As hospitals faced a crisis because of overflowing Covid patients, other services like oncology, surgery, HIV/AIDs and tuberculosis suffered immensely. Studies will, over time, unravel the loss of human life occasioned by these conditions as our focus turns to the new virus.

Every doctor has a story to tell about this period. Many will tell you that few, if any, patients survived intubation and ventilatory support after suffering severe COVID-19. I have pored over data from many hospitals; the scenario is the same—almost all intubated patients died.

One Monday morning, I was called into one of the nearby hospitals to urgently review a 56-year-old gentleman who had checked into the hospital with difficulty in breathing. I made a detour into the hospital on my way to work.

The resident doctor ran me through the history: a known diabetic with poor glycaemic control who started experiencing fevers and night sweats five days before. He had muscle and joint aches. He self-medicated on antimalarials for three days, but the symptoms progressed.

I looked at the gentleman. He was covered in sweat, panting, and unconscious. He was receiving two litres of oxygen via nasal prongs. I reached for the pulse oximeter. His oxygen saturation stood at an ominous 46%. We were staring at respiratory failure and death unless something was done urgently.

I auscultated his lungs—there were widespread coarse crackles like shuffling feet on dry grass. All his lung fields appeared ravaged by the disease. I recommended to the son that he needed urgent admission to the Intensive Care Unit (ICU). Only that there was trouble. At that time, ICU beds in the country numbered less than 100. By the time the COVID-19 virus had been subdued in 2022, the country had over 500 ICU beds. It took a crisis to awaken this reality.

After much persuasion, the trauma ward in one of the public hospitals was turned into an ICU, fitted with oxygen and ventilator machines. The patient was admitted there.

At the beginning of the pandemic, various drugs were repurposed for the treatment of COVID-19. Studies emerged showing the efficacy of azithromycin. This was followed by hydroxychloroquine and ivermectin. No sooner had they started being used than more robust data came out that they did not affect the morbidity and mortality of patients with COVID-19. Indeed, they even appeared to have negative effects compared to the placebo. The only drug that showed efficacy and reduced hospitalisation and deaths among patients needing oxygen was the steroid dexamethasone[5].

So, we intubated the patient and put him on dexamethasone over and above other supportive treatment and waited, not knowing whether he would pull through or not. He slipped into a coma that lasted for

---

[5] Medication that provides relief for inflamed areas of the body. It is used to treat a number of different conditions, such as inflammation (swelling), severe allergies, adrenal problems, arthritis, asthma, blood or bone marrow problems, kidney problems, skin conditions, and flare-ups of multiple sclerosis.

fourteen days. His oxygen levels fluctuated until the eighth day, when we noted a decrease in his oxygen requirements. We slowly turned down the ventilator settings until we weaned him off the vent on the fourteenth day.

"Where am I?" He asked, visibly confused.

He looked around at the beeping machines and may have realised that he was in the hospital. Later, when I met him, he told me that two weeks of his life were a blur. He thinks he just slept and woke up, or worse still, he was dead and resurrected. We discharged him for home-based oxygen. The family requested that I follow up on him three times a week. His progress was encouraging. Within three weeks, he was breathing well on ambient air and had almost fully recovered, except for a slight cough and fatigue that would occasionally assail him whenever he took a few steps.

He was the first patient in our hospital to be intubated in a makeshift ICU, but the only one who survived the ventilator and made a full recovery. Other critical patients who went this route would die during intubation, treatment, or, inexplicably, would seem to have improved until the day of extubation, when they would suffer fatal cardiac arrest.

One excruciating case I will never forget is of a close friend who was intubated but was fully conscious. He made a remarkable recovery, and every day I saw him, he would scribble his complaints for the day and his progress on a piece of paper. I was optimistic that he would be a story of victory until the day of extubation, when he suffered a fatal cardiac arrest. Not even our prolonged CPR would revive him. I have kept the written pieces of paper as evidence of hope and strength in the throes of death. It was devastating.

Eventually, vaccines arrived and calmed the raging storm, although they met their own sceptics. I remember being called to see one medic who had severe respiratory distress. Upon questioning him about vaccination, he told me that he had not bothered to be vaccinated but would do so upon discharge. He progressed to severe respiratory failure and eventually died. I don't know whether the vaccine would have saved him, but I reasoned that his fighting chance would have been much better if he had been vaccinated.

By the time the lockdown was lifted, entire populations had been affected. Unlike the bubonic plague, which is spread by fleas from infected rats and primarily affects lower social classes, COVID-19 did not discriminate among social classes, being a respiratory virus. Many prominent people died, including leaders of some countries.

Even the biggest fires must eventually be extinguished. We are now in the post-COVID-19 era, where the transmission rate has flattened. Scientists believe that mutating variants of COVID-19, especially the Omicron variant, may have infected almost the entire world population, creating herd immunity that shields the population from further spread.

It is interesting how the world moves on from crises. At the national level, things continue as if nothing had happened. Perhaps it is at the individual and family level where the pain remains, the wounds fester, and the scars as they remember loved ones who perished in the pandemic.

And there will be another pandemic, but no one knows when it will occur. Whether humanity will be ready to face it remains unknown.

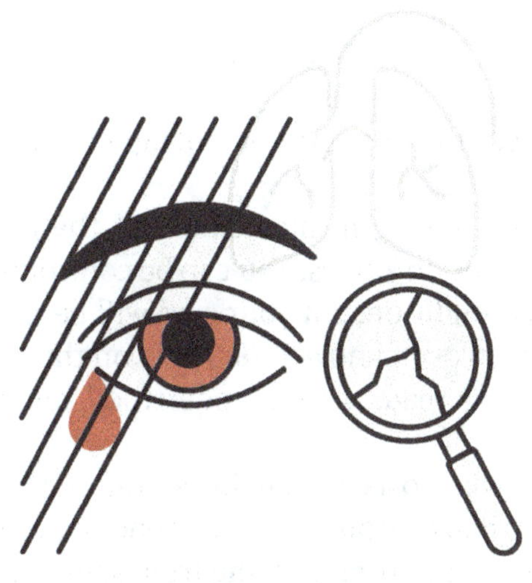

CHAPTER 8

HIDDEN IN PLAIN SIGHT

THE TRANSITION FROM MEDICAL SCHOOL to actual hospital medicine can be difficult and nearly impossible for some newly graduated doctors. From being a learner or innocent bystander in a ward round and handing over instruments during surgeries to being at the steering wheel, nothing works during a medical internship other than the experience of actually doing it.

The brain is a complicated organ. It receives stimuli from the environment through the various senses and, after a complex integration process, gives commands to the body. These commands may take the form of actions, answers, or outright ignoring the stimulus.

There is a saying in medicine that the eyes only see what the brain knows. You can be confronted with an obvious condition, but your eyes will be fixated on what you think you know. It depends on the intersection of what is read, what is understood, and what is practised.

Medical diagnosis is usually a conundrum—it is learnt from books, from past experiences, from divine intervention, and from learning from seniors.

I was posted to a rural hospital for my one-year mandatory internship in 2011. I knew what to expect: long working hours, inadequate study time, running around handling emergencies, and being the fall guy in case things went wrong. Internship remains a cruel initiation into medical practice that up-and-coming doctors must endure.

I remember during my thirteen-week obstetrics and gynaecology rotation at the university, one of the conditions we were cautioned to be always wary of was ectopic pregnancy. "A woman dying of ectopic pregnancy under your watch is a criminal offence," I remember one of our consultants insisting. Yet this condition appears deceptively simple, but is actually difficult to detect.

On this Friday night, I retired to the small hospital call room for a quick nap. It was a long day spent performing caesarean deliveries.

Caesarean delivery is the first major operation a medical officer intern learns. It is taught quickly and decisively, and once it is learnt, the senior doctor sighs with relief, for you will not need to call them late in the night for emergency deliveries.

I received a call from the hospital emergency department about a 19-year-old girl who had reported to the facility with vaginal bleeding.

Perhaps due to experience, I assumed this was an incomplete abortion. There was an uncanny tendency for incomplete abortions to present to the hospital on Friday evenings. We later found out that professionals in backstreet clinics assisting women to procure this service would advise them to come to the facility (which was the main referral facility in the area) by the end of the week if vaginal bleeding did not stop.

In Kenya, almost 500, 000 abortions are conducted annually, translating to an abortion rate of 48 per 1,000 women of reproductive age (15-49 years). Notably, over 70% of these are carried by personnel without proper qualifications. It is no wonder that unsafe abortions leading to death from bleeding, pulmonary embolism and sepsis account for up to 20% of maternal mortalities in Kenya.

The 2010 constitution bans abortion except in very exceptional circumstances when the life of the mother is in danger. This means abortions shouldn't be carried out in hospitals or legally licensed clinics.

But does that mean women don't procure abortion services in Kenya?

While this debate remains unending and opinions remain bitterly divided, the truth of the matter is that this has created a lacuna for backstreet, illegal clinics, manned by unqualified personnel, to offer these services, often to the detriment of the clients.

"You will first go to the police station and obtain an abstract and Occurrence Book (OB) number for attempting to procure an illegal abortion!" I barked at one weak-looking woman on a cold Friday night.

My mind could not reconcile itself with how I was obligated to complete an incomplete abortion, whose indication I did not know. Apparently, the performers of these dark acts would advise patients to come to the government hospital within three days if the bleeding did not subside. Most women opted to wait out the week and seek care on Friday evenings. It was the duty of the poor medical officer to perform Manual Vacuum Aspirations on the patients.

The woman I threatened to have locked up was anaemic from prolonged bleeding and was shivering.

I don't know how the case reached the medical superintendent. He called me.

"Dr Bundi, have you read the ethical principles of medicine?"

"Yes, sir," I replied.

"In that case, then, if a murderer comes to you, and in one of his murderous escapades, he has sustained a gunshot to the thigh, do you lock him up or first save his life?" he asked me.

"I should save his life first, sir," I meekly replied.

"So, what's the difference with the woman you are about to condemn? Can you go ahead and perform the MVA before any other stories?"

The ethical principles of medicine are four:

Beneficence—the duty to do good.

Autonomy—respect for the right of the patient to self-determination. As long as the patient is of sound mind and they don't threaten the health of the larger population, they retain the right to accept or refuse a medical intervention, even when this decision can lead to certain death. This is famously summarised in the ancient dictum, 'Every human being of adult years and sound mind has a right to determine what shall be done with his own body'.

Non-maleficence—first, do no harm. Whatever you offer to the patient should not harm the patient. If an intervention causes more harm than good, it is better to leave the patient to wallow in their infirmity. Even when dealing with a criminal, you first treat him and let other legal and criminal justice consequences take their course later. Summarised effectively, non-maleficence means do not kill, do not cause pain or suffering, do not incapacitate, do not cause offence, and do not deprive others of the goods of life.

Justice—treating every patient as a sentient being worthy of honour, without discrimination. After all, the human body is the same, and the basic anatomo-physiological and biochemical underpinnings of the human body transcend class and status.

I reasoned that if doctors, having been the first legal professionals to encounter these events, cannot report them for punishment, then who will?

Again, a look at the criminal justice system, with its intricacies and complexities, would suggest that no sane doctor would leave medical practice to spend their days on the cold benches of the courts giving evidence. Often, as in other cases, the prosecution may lose files, lose interest in the case, or even turn against you. Perhaps the way to beat this is to turn the taps on the very act that leads to unintended pregnancies. Or does this offer enough justification for legalising abortion? The debate will always veer into religious, cultural, superstitious, and even moral dimensions. It is a difficult debate.

I might have drifted back to sleep because the next time the call came, it had a note of urgency.

"Daktari, we need your opinion here. It may be an MVA."

MVA means Manual Vacuum Aspiration, an improvised procedure for managing incomplete miscarriages and blighted ovum. It involves using a manual suction pump to aspirate uterine contents. The cessation of vaginal bleeding and the appearance of bubbles in the syringe reservoir is the signal that all products of conception have been evacuated. This method has been hailed for its simplicity and speed compared to the older method, which involved curettage of the endometrium to remove the products of conception. Curettage usually causes abrasions and scars in the uterus, predisposing mothers to ectopic pregnancies. Others would experience abnormal implantation of the placenta in inappropriate areas, leading to antepartum haemorrhage in their subsequent pregnancies.

I stepped out into the cold night and headed for the emergency department. It was 11:00 PM. The hospital was unusually quiet, except for the emergency department, where patients thronged for help. It was in the middle of the rainy season.

The senior clinician took me through the patient's details, who lay on the couch with her worried mother by her side: A 19-year-old college student who was well until earlier in the day when she presented with mild vaginal bleeding and cramping abdominal pains. She was seen in our facility that afternoon and sent home on analgesic medication.

"Pregnancy test?" I asked no one in particular.

It had not been done.

The girl protested that she could not have been pregnant as she had no sexual relations with a man. Not recently, and not at all, she insisted.

I ignored her protests and called the laboratory technologist. A rapid test result was positive for pregnancy.

"I swear I have never slept with a man," she protested, with a look of innocence on her face.

Her mother looked at her, bewildered. I looked at her absent-mindedly, exhausted by the long day I had endured.

"Then you will be the second one after Mary, the mother of Jesus," the senior clinician who had called me shouted.

I restrained a smile.

I explained to the mother that we needed to perform a speculum examination to visualise the source of the bleeding.

The girl wiggled and winced in pain as I advanced the speculum. I encountered a thick hymen, perhaps an indication that she was a virgin, as she said. The bleeding was minimal, and I did not visualise the *cervical os*[6] due to the discomfort it caused, but also due to a conclusion I had already made in my mind that she had procured an abortion.

I turned to the mother and suggested we discharge the girl home to come back the following day, when we would examine her again and perform the MVA procedure once the cervix was dilated.

"The girls of today are funny. She wants us to believe that she miraculously conceived," I mumbled to my colleague as I scribbled on her hospital card and handed it to the mother.

I checked around the emergency department for any other cases that needed my review. Most of the cases were medical in nature—alcoholic gastritis, assault cases, delirium, convulsions. The medical officer intern rotating in internal medicine was having a long night. In the antenatal ward, there was no indication I would be called for a caesarean delivery in the next five hours. All mothers in labour were in their early stages, and none had features of foetal distress.

I thanked the heavens for the day and buried myself in the hospital bed sheets.

I don't know how long I had been sleeping when I woke up to the incessant beeping of my phone. Initially, I dreamed someone was calling me, but when it

---

[6] the opening or mouth of the cervix, the lower part of the uterus, divided into the internal os (opening into the uterus) and the external os (opening into the vagina).

didn't stop, I threw off the blankets and jumped out of bed.

"The same girl has come back. The mother says she collapsed in the bathroom."

Sleep left my mind almost in an instant, and I felt a flash of fear cut through my chest.

What could be happening? Why would she have symptoms of severe anaemia, yet the vaginal bleeding was negligible? When I had seen her earlier, she had only used two pads since the bleeding started, which was not alarming for excessive bleeding.

Still, no answer seemed to form in my mind, even as I raced down the pavement to the emergency department.

This time, I was humbled, humbled by having missed something or having sent the beleaguered mother and girl home for a second time in less than 10 hours without a solution.

I checked her conjunctivae—she was *paper white*; a phrase we use to describe someone with critically low blood levels. Yet her haemoglobin on her first encounter in the hospital Friday afternoon was 12.

I turned to the clinician, who sat at the corner of the room, his right hand to his cheek. He also seemed to be thinking hard, but no solution seemed forthcoming.

I reviewed the pelvic ultrasound performed earlier, and it only showed endometrial thickening. Eerily, it did not show a foetal pole or products of conception. This was not startling to me, for if a miscarriage were underway, the ultrasound would have missed the obvious.

The answer to the many questions seemed to hit me like a thunderbolt. A sudden realisation washed over me, and I thought a diagnosis had been revealed to me. If she is not bleeding vaginally, where is the blood going? I asked myself.

When a doctor sobers up, he goes back to the basics. First, principles of anatomy, physiology, and other basic sciences can help you work your way to a diagnosis.

That's when it dawned on me that I was possibly dealing with an ectopic pregnancy. I quickly examined her abdomen. Her right iliac fossa [7]was tender. Something was happening there.

I called the theatre to prepare for an emergency laparotomy. I asked the nurse on duty to authorise the ambulance to pick up my immediate senior, a medical officer who lived in a town five kilometres away.

There was, however, a monumental challenge: Our hospital blood bank was dry.

The heavens had opened up. Thunder and lightning disrupted the cold night, adding to the gloom that engulfed me. I was faced with two options: to take the risk and proceed to the theatre even with her critically low haemoglobin or initiate a referral to the national hospital, about 100 kilometres away. The nurse on the night shift had joined us in the room. She reasoned that a referral was more dangerous; it was unlikely that this girl would make it alive. We were

---

[7] The concave, inner surface of the ilium (part of the hip bone), also known as the smooth hollow on the medial surface of the iliac blade.

better off operating on her and prayed that blood loss from the operation would be minimal.

Ever since I qualified as a doctor, I have maintained the argument that young patients should be treated with utmost care and thoroughness. They are the pillars of a society. This does not mean that I don't apply myself completely to the care of older people. I do. But I reckon that a 19-year-old, with a whole life ahead of her, requires greater thought than a 90-year-old.

My senior medical officer arrived within a few minutes. He looked at the girl, who lay weak in bed. His reaction encouraged me. We would make it.

As the anaesthetist injected medicine into her vein, I was busy scrubbing. My hands were shaking as I followed the surgical steps for hand washing. I may have missed some minuscule steps, but I gowned and gloved, ready for the procedure.

She was already asleep, her soft abdomen exposed. With my supervisor as the assistant, we dabbed the skin with iodine, and when we were sure she was well sterilised, we cleaned the area again with saline.

The circulating nurse performed a count of the gauze, a procedure designed to ensure that gauze was not left in the abdomen.

Just as I moved the instruments and picked up surgical blade number 23 to make the Pfannenstiel incision[8], the nurse stopped me and offered to pray.

---

[8] Also known as a bikini incision, is a transverse (horizontal) surgical incision in the lower abdomen, commonly used for caesarean sections and other pelvic surgeries, made approximately 2 finger-breadths above the pubic symphysis (the joint between the two pelvic bones) and extends towards the anterior superior iliac spines (points on the outside of the pelvis).

She fervently prayed for God to spare the life of this beautiful girl and to give us clarity of thought. She prayed against surgical complications and excessive bleeding. She bound the spirit of death. She uplifted us all. The prayer took a protracted course but greatly calmed the operating team.

I made the cut at 2:15 AM on Saturday. After a careful dissection of the layers of the anterior abdomen, we reached the peritoneal cavity[9]. The evidence was glaring before our own eyes—a massive collection of blood which, when aspirated, was over three litres.

We flashed the cavity with warm saline and searched for the source of the bleeding. The right fallopian tube had ruptured. It still sent blood in spurts, which threatened to extinguish this young life with exsanguination[10].

We promptly reached for the fallopian tube, ligated the bleeder and performed a salpingectomy (the surgical removal of one or both fallopian tubes) on the affected tube. The bleeding stopped. Our hopes rose.

We flashed the cavity again with warm saline. This time, the surgical field was clean, with no evidence of further bleeding.

As we closed the abdomen, I looked at the monitor. The blood pressure was holding steady. The oxygen saturations were steady. The electrocardiogram (ECG)

---

[9] The space within the abdomen, between the visceral and parietal layers of the peritoneum (a serous membrane that lines the abdominal wall), containing a small amount of lubricating fluid.

[10] A critical amount of blood in a short amount of time, leading to a state of shock and potentially death.

tracing was still in sinus rhythm. Trouble seemed to have evaded us; rather, we had evaded trouble.

It was early morning when she was wheeled to the ward. I kept vigil, checking her vitals. The covering nurse had, by this time, raised an ambulance to fetch blood from a regional transfusion centre about 50 kilometres away. By the time she was fully awake, she was being transfused.

I was applying the lessons learned during my undergraduate obstetrics and gynaecology rotation. Ectopic pregnancies are easy to deal with surgically, but 10–20 per cent of them will cause death because of their subtle presentation and the inability of the doctor to connect the dots quickly. Worryingly, ultrasound imaging of the abdomen is not 100 per cent sensitive; it will miss some of the cases.

Over the course of the next few days, the girl made good progress and was on her feet by the second day. I made a point of dropping by her bed frequently to check on her.

"*Haki,* Daktari, I never did it." She told me one day.

"You didn't do what?" I asked, bewildered.

"I know you guys blame me for having sex, but I swear I did not." She seemed sure of herself.

"Forget about that," I swatted her away.

She insisted on explaining what had happened.

She had just joined college. She was living on her own when her high school boyfriend visited. They huddled together and watched a movie. The chemistry increased over the course of hours, and they found themselves kissing. There was no penetration, but it is possible that ejaculation occurred at the introitus[11].

It was a rare case of virgin pregnancy. It was another obstetric lesson for me as I left the room even more bemused.

[11] In the context of the female reproductive system, the vaginal introitus is the external opening of the vaginal canal.

CHAPTER 9

SERENDIPITY

IT WAS 24 DECEMBER 2019 when I received a call from my colleague, a consultant obstetrician in the teaching hospital. During this time of the year, most professions have closed for Christmas festivities, save for healthcare workers, whose work does not recognise holidays and festivities. She was managing a 20-year-old primigravida[12] who came a day earlier with intractable seizures. She had given birth to a live male infant. My colleague had made a diagnosis

[12] A woman who is pregnant for the first time.

of eclampsia, a serious pregnancy complication where a pregnant or postpartum woman experiences seizures, but the presentation and laboratory features did not add up. Despite the incongruent clinic-laboratory features, she administered an infusion of magnesium sulphate, hoping to extinguish the seizures. Instead, the intensity and frequency increased. Another colleague suggested a loading dose of the anticonvulsant drug phenytoin. She received three loading doses, but the seizures were unrelenting. By the time I was called, she was in *status epilepticus*, a state of continuous seizures that can be rapidly fatal if unchecked.

I hopped into the car, deep in thought. A list of differential diagnoses ran through my mind as I started the car.

The hospital CT scan machine was out of service, meaning there was no way we would know if she had suffered a stroke or had a brain tumour. It was during a holiday weekend, with most private facilities closed. The region had no functional neurophysiology laboratory that could have further aided the diagnosis. Helping this young woman was going to be down to instincts, first principles, and serendipity, as I learned later that day.

When working as a doctor in resource-constrained settings, you rely on first principles to help the sick. First principles, in this case, imply the application of basic science concepts in medicine, ranging from human anatomy and medical physiology to clinical sciences. You see a patient presenting with left-sided chest pain. You must thoroughly examine every aspect of the history to determine whether the pain is cardiac, pericardial, pleural, muscular, or skeletal. Worse still, the pain can be psychogenic.

If the application of these principles does not produce a clear diagnosis, you must imagine the worst as you hope for the best. It is, therefore, unforgivable that you will treat left-sided chest pain as mere muscle pain when it could be a fatal heart attack. It is better to treat a patient for a heart attack that is eventually found not to be there than not treat a patient for a heart attack that is there. This medical principle draws heavily on statistical sciences regarding alpha and beta errors. To put it briefly, it is better to acquit a known terrorist than hang an innocent man.

This was the second case that came down to pure instinctual thinking and a brave application of sound principles.

In June 2019, a 41-year-old gentleman was referred to my private office with rapidly progressing weakness in both upper and lower limbs. Earlier in the day, he underwent a Magnetic Resonance Imaging (MRI) scan of the brain, which revealed a deep cortical lesion infiltrating the basal ganglia and capsular region on the left side.

The basal ganglia are a deep-seated brain organ that modulates movement. It fine-tunes and dampens movements, enabling someone to accelerate or decelerate without clumsiness. Failure of this part of the brain produces Parkinsonism, a syndrome attended by sluggishness, tremors, rigidity of the joints, and eventually trouble initiating movements. A patient with this syndrome will walk with a stoop, having slurred speech and reduced eye blinks, and when advanced, they can experience severe freezing of gait with festination, an involuntary tendency to take short, accelerating steps when walking.

I admitted this man to one of the main faith-based hospitals. The family requested that I follow up on him every day until he recovered. I was not sure of recovery because the radiologist had made a discouraging conclusion in the MRI report: *infiltrative lesion of the capsule-ganglionic region of the brain, indicative of an infiltrating brain tumour, with a high likelihood of a lymphoma.*

The location of the lesion deep within the brain, as well as its infiltrative pattern, meant that surgical removal was out of the question. An attempt at excision would definitely mean damage to many structures along the surgical path and removal of parts of the basal ganglia.

I explained to the relatives the predicament we were facing and that the only option available was to give the patient steroids to reduce brain swelling around the lesion. If it continued to grow, the patient would lapse into a coma and eventually die.

By the second day, the man had lapsed into a coma. Our infusion of dexamethasone did little to stem his rapid decline, which accelerated into a deep coma within five days. We inserted a tube through the nose to the stomach for feeding and instituted other nursing measures to avoid pressure sores, deep vein thrombosis, and hypostatic pneumonia.

As agreed, I dutifully reviewed the patient every morning, noting little progress. I had reached a point of desperation. It is disheartening to see a patient go down, as relatives look up to you for answers. You are acutely aware of the deficiencies surrounding the case, but the duty of care restrains you from giving up entirely. After all, if the doctor gives up, what happens to the family and relatives?

In the sinking Titanic of disease, the captain, who happens to be the doctor, must be the last person to leave the ship after ensuring the safety of everyone else on board. If all lifeboats have been dished out, the captain must, with courage and conviction, jump into the sea and die a hero.

One morning, I felt inspired to perform a fresh physical examination of the comatose gentleman. The ward nurse assisted me in exposing him from head to toe.

He was sweaty, cachexic[13], and in a deep coma.

I followed the rule book for neurological examination: Start with higher functions. In this case, he was in a coma, with a scale of six out of 15. Next, I checked the face and eyes for any clues. None. I flexed his neck to check for any stiffening. The neck was stiff. This gave me a slight opening upon which to cling. The body provides the doctor with clues to disease, clues that can hold the key to diagnosis and eventual salvation of the same body.

He had quadriplegia (paralysis of all four limbs), but tellingly, his deep tendon reflexes were preserved.

---

[13] a severe metabolic syndrome characterized by unintentional weight loss and muscle mass loss.

I stroked the sole of the foot with my pen. The toes fanned out, yet another clue of where the problem lay.

I left his bedside that morning, having formed an examination diagnosis of meningitis syndrome. In this hospital, there are no studies of cerebrospinal fluid to confirm meningitis.

A thought crossed my mind. Could I be dealing with tuberculous meningitis?

For centuries, tuberculosis has been a challenging disease. It has consumed millions and remains one of the most difficult conditions to diagnose. Doctors call it the great masquerader because it can masquerade as any other condition. It can affect any part of the body except hair and nails.

One of the 19th century's prominent physicians extolled his students that no patient should be left to die before being given the option of TB treatment. The eminent scientist Robert Koch isolated the bacterium that causes TB and proudly presented his findings to the Society of Physiology in Berlin in 1882.

Before this discovery, TB had been labelled the Great Consumption because of the devastation it visited on its hapless victims before killing them. Benjamin Marten, an English physician, was the first to postulate, in his publication, 'A New Theory of Consumptions', that TB could be caused by 'wonderfully minute living creatures', which, once they had gained a foothold in the body, could generate the lesions and symptoms of the disease. He stated, moreover, 'It may be therefore very likely that by a habitual lying in the same bed with a consumptive patient, constantly eating and drinking with him, or by very frequently conversing so nearly as to draw in part of the breath he emits from the lungs, a consumption may be caught by a sound person ... I imagine that slightly conversing with consumptive patients is seldom or never sufficient to catch the disease'. This publication may have seemed postulatory, but it provided valuable insights into how this bacterium is spread from one person to another.

By the early 1800s, Europeans and Americans described TB as 'Captain of All These Men of Death', because it accounted for the deaths of one in every four people.

Despite rapid advances in the knowledge of this ancient organism, it was not until the 1950s that treatment for TB was discovered.

TB is now known to be a curable disease, but its presentation and difficulties in diagnosis make it one of the top five killers in the global south today.

Medical history has fascinated me since my early days of training. Having devoured works of medieval, Renaissance, and industrial-age scientists and writers on TB, I have made a conscious decision to treat TB whenever I rationally suspect it and whenever it makes clinical sense, particularly in the absence of another confirmed diagnosis.

It is little wonder that when I prescribed anti-TB treatment for this gentleman, the public health officers manning the TB desk in the Meru County Department of Health hesitated in providing the medications. They wanted microbiological evidence of TB infection in the patient. None was forthcoming.

I called the head of the desk and explained my scientific, historical and economic basis for this decision. He seemed to agree with me, but complained about rigid national guidelines that demanded evidence of TB infection before the provision of medications. I convinced him that diseases don't read books and that guidelines are not the end in themselves but must be applied in the context of the patient. He eventually agreed to dispense the medications.

The gentleman stayed in a coma for a further three weeks as we administered TB medicine through the nasogastric tube.

During one of the visits, I noticed that he would bring his hands up to resist whenever I rubbed his sternum. It was the first sign that he was waking up. His progress was slow and protracted, but by the seventh week, he tried removing the nasogastric tube and would open his eyes whenever we called his name.

The progress was uplifting. We called in the physical rehabilitation team to administer exercises to strengthen his muscles. After eleven weeks in the hospital, I discharged him for home-based care. He was wheelchair-bound but making steady progress.

During subsequent visits to my private office, his progress was unmistakable. At three months, I requested a follow-up brain MRI, which showed significant shrinkage of the mass lesion in the brain. By the sixth month, the brain lesion had all but disappeared.

I saw him at eight months, unaccompanied, as he walked sprightly to my office. It was a stunning testament to the power of serendipity and, perhaps, the uncanny ability to clutch at the slightest straw during a storm.

But now here I was, faced with a young lady in a state of continuous convulsions, which we medically call *status epilepticus*. Peninah, as the 20-year-old lady was called, was a college student who had come home pregnant after closing school in September 2019. She attended only one antenatal clinic. The next time she came to the hospital, she was violently convulsing. Labour was induced, and after a perfect partograph[14], she delivered a live male infant who weighed 3.2 kilograms.

Her mother stood beside her, praying fervently as wave upon wave of convulsion assailed her. A drip of anticonvulsant medication was running down her vein, but this did little to stem the waves of seizures that came every few minutes.

I shone a light on her pupils. They were equal and normally reacted to light. I checked for any weakness on the face and the limbs. None was apparent. I flexed the neck to check for any sign of meningism. The neck was supple. Another seizure episode attacked her.

Asking yourself rational questions can sometimes open the deep recesses of your brain to answers hidden within the subconscious.

I asked myself, *if this young lady does not have eclampsia, what else can present with such violent seizures at the time of delivery or late in her pregnancy?*

---

[14] A labour monitoring tool that uses a graphical record of key data (like cervical dilation, foetal heart rate, and vital signs) to track labour progression and identify potential complications in a mother and her baby.

The first answer that came to my mind changed the game. Sometimes, a doctor knows when they have clinched the diagnosis. A jigsaw puzzle fits. It is like having a hundred keys trying to open one lock. You know when the right key has entered the keyhole. The feeling is unmistakable. It is a revelation.

Peninah had cerebral sinus thrombosis, a condition that occurs when a blood clot forms in the brain's venous sinuses, potentially leading to swelling, bleeding, and stroke-like symptoms. There was no scan to confirm, and no D-dimer test to increase the diagnostic probability, but I informed the medical officer who was recording my findings that this was the diagnosis we would work with.

We fashioned an infusion of the anticoagulant heparin and disconnected the anticonvulsant. Heparin had not run for five minutes when seizures stopped. She regained consciousness, and the waves of headaches dramatically disappeared.

Her improvement proved dramatic. From the initiation of heparin until her discharge two days later, she experienced no headaches, no seizures, and no disturbance in consciousness.

That evening, I revealed the events of the day to my wife, who is also a medical doctor.

"That diagnosis was divine revelation," she remarked.

I could barely disagree with her. Perhaps the only addition to her remark is that such a diagnosis cannot be revealed without applying rational thinking and sound principles of science.

"Exactly. God does not reveal things to anybody. Even prophets had to ascend the mountains of God for revelation. They had to read the signs and wonders of God," she concluded.

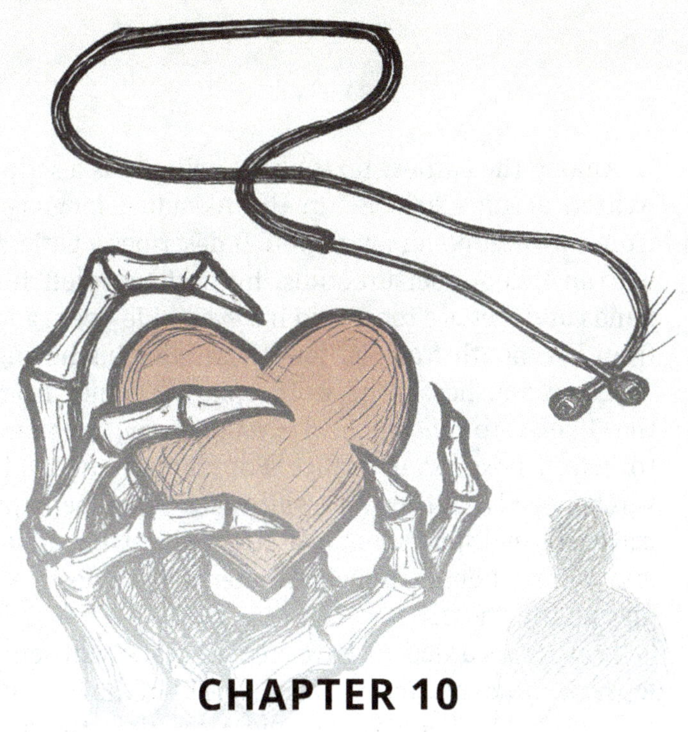

CHAPTER 10

ONE FRIGHTENING DISEASE

FEW DISEASES ELICIT FEAR AND wonder in the onlooker and the caregiver than epilepsy. Witnessing a generalised epileptic attack, in all its fury and wonder, is like witnessing the throes of death. Indeed, many relatives of a patient who has had an epileptic seizure will think that the victim was resisting death itself. The violent motor activity and the attendant symptoms that come upon an individual during a convulsive episode are apocalyptic, traumatising, and sometimes unforgettable to the onlooker.

Among the earliest texts about epilepsy is a script written around 2000 BC in the Akkadian language from the Mesopotamian region. It describes a patient with an epileptic seizure; thus, 'his neck turns left, his hands and feet are tense and his eyes wide open, and from his mouth froth is flowing without his having any consciousness'. The word epilepsy comes from the Greek verb *epilambanein* (επιλαμβάνειν), meaning to 'seize', 'possess', or 'afflict'. For many centuries, it was believed that this was a spiritual disease, perhaps caused by evil spirits that overpowered the individual and caused them extreme movements and a desire to give up the ghost.

Jesus is recorded to have healed a boy with epilepsy, who was seized by 'an evil spirit' in the book of Luke 9:39-42. This episode vividly describes the travails of a young boy whose father knelt before Jesus in earnest supplication: "Lord, have mercy on my son, for he has seizures, and he suffers terribly. For he often falls into the fire, and often into the water." The association of epilepsy with evil spirits is reminiscent of the common belief of the day. The semiology of the seizure is further described, 'and behold, a spirit seizes him, and he suddenly cries out. It convulses him so that he foams at the mouth, and shatters him, and will hardly leave him'.

Even today, it is not uncommon to come across epilepsy patients who have suffered terrible burns, injuries due to falls, and near-drowning episodes. This is despite the advances in medicine.

If you have ever witnessed a generalised seizure, you would also agree that the sheer manifestation can easily be regarded as an actual seizure by spirits. The person will suddenly stand up, as if jolted by an evil force, turn their head in one direction and effectively become frozen. With a shrill cry, they will fall with a thud and stiffen all their limbs. They will roll their eyes, foam at the mouth and jerk their limbs. Oftentimes, the patient will be oblivious to what's happening. The scared parent or witness will tell you that they thought the patient was actually giving up their ghost.

Hippocrates, the Father of Medicine, was among the first early-day physicians to write that epilepsy was not a sacred disease but rather a physical perturbation in the brain, manifesting in a violent manner. Since the Renaissance and the Industrial Age, remarkable progress has been made in the study of epilepsy. The brain networks that generate seizures, the aetiology of the seizures, and the semiology have been well described with advancements in medicine. What remains to be tackled is the many intriguing ways it manifests and, conversely, the many other conditions that can be mistaken for epilepsy. This is what epileptologists refer to as 'mimics', borderland and chameleons. The untrained eye will believe that everything that faints or seizes is epilepsy. Nothing could be further from the truth. Not all that faints or convulses is epilepsy, and not all epileptics seize or faint!

I have handled many cases of epilepsy mimics, but one case stuck in my head. Several physicians had already assessed this 12-year-old girl for a seizure disorder and were using supramaximal doses of two anti-seizure medications. Yet, she continued experiencing alarming seizure episodes that left her parents worried and confused. She had undergone numerous diagnostic tests, which returned negative results.

She came into my office accompanied by her father. The description of the main event was almost characteristically that of a seizure, only that the aural event had the slightest hint that we could be dealing with a different problem.

She described a severe frontal headache that almost blinded her. Then she would feel the 'seizure' coming, upon which she would quickly sit or look for a place to lie. She didn't know what followed, but her classmates and teachers witnessed violent, jerky movements that would progress for several minutes. She would be foaming at the mouth. Her eyes would be closed.

Most of the time, this would be succeeded by a deep, unarousable sleep, which persisted until she was taken to the nearest hospital. A saline drip and an injection of analgesic medication would wake her up almost instantaneously.

"What happens when she wakes up?" I asked the father.

"She looks around the room, disoriented, and demands to know where she is. She will then complain of a severe frontal headache, which is only calmed by an injection."

Just then, she complained of a severe headache.

"I can't see!" She exclaimed.

We calmly lifted her into the bed, and I asked the father to calm down.

I observed an uncoordinated series of jerky movements in the limbs, accompanied by frothing of saliva. I quickly called the neurophysiology technician to prepare the electroencephalography (EEG) machine[15] to place wires on her scalp and record the supposed seizure activity.

I held one of her legs, which was actively flailing. It stopped activity and shifted to the left leg.

I was convinced we were dealing with another condition, but not epilepsy.

It took about 20 minutes for her to regain consciousness. She appeared a little dazed, but soon cleared up and was normal again. I asked her whether she knew the attack was coming. Yes, she felt it coming.

Electroencephalography (EEG) is a recording of the electrical activity in the brain. This electrical activity is generated by the firing of neuronal cells, which produce an electric field that can be detected by placing wires on the scalp and using an amplifier to record the impulses. It is not a fool-proof method as it can miss deep-seated epileptic foci, but it will rarely miss the diagnosis in an actively convulsing individual.

The EEG recording was eerily normal in this girl. I looked at her MRI scans again. There was no hint of structural abnormality in the brain. Her blood works were clean.

---

[15] a device that measures and records the electrical activity of the brain, typically using electrodes placed on the scalp, to help diagnose and monitor various neurological conditions.

I turned to the last roll of the dice: her psychosocial well-being. She was in a boarding school, having been transferred there from a day school eight months earlier. The transition was difficult for her. She missed home and found the school food bland, the routines punishing, and the teachers too rigid.

Looking at the father, I declared that this girl had psychogenic nonepileptic seizures brought about by an adjustment disorder in school. The change of environment and routine had left her traumatised. Her young brain could not process the problem or connect the dots to understand the root cause of the issue.

He did not immediately believe me, but I insisted that the cure for her problem was to change her school. I drafted a letter to the father to assist him in enrolling her in a day school. We agreed I would see her again in one month.

I did not see her again for four months. When a patient skips an appointment, doctors are inclined to conclude two things: either the patient has recovered and sees no need for a further appointment, or the patient was less impressed by the encounter and has sought care elsewhere. I assumed the latter.

Four months later, I met the father at a social function. He looked relaxed and happy. He pulled me aside and thanked me profusely for saving his daughter. From the day I wrote the transfer letter, the convulsive episodes ceased completely.

"She has been free of medications for four months and has never complained of headaches, visual blurring or fainting episodes," he told me.

More disturbing than the above case of an epilepsy mimic is a manifestation of epilepsy that resembles mimics more than epilepsy itself. Epileptologists call them chameleons.

Joy was a 16-year-old high school girl who developed a sudden onset of unprovoked laughter. The first time it happened, she was in class. The teacher did not take it kindly, but Joy did not seem perturbed by the teacher's protests. She laughed so hard that she almost rolled on the floor.

Her seatmate had noted uncommon drowsiness in Joy. On this day, she had slumped asleep on her desk, and when she woke up, she was laughing.

"What is funny?" The alarmed teacher asked.

She went on laughing. The class joined her.

She was later summoned to the deputy principal's office, where she was severely reprimanded for her unbecoming behaviour. The deputy principal and her teacher were bewildered that she looked innocent and seemed to have forgotten her transgressions.

Only later, during the school holidays, did her mother hear an uncommon laugh coming from her room in the dead of night. She burst into Joy's room and found her in bed, laughing at nothing.

When they sought medical attention, nothing was forthcoming. Her quality of sleep deteriorated, punctuated by daytime sleepiness. There was a problem somewhere.

"Everything emanates from the brain," offered one physician to the worried mother.

"I advise that we do a brain MRI scan."

The scan revealed a hypothalamic hamartoma, a benign (non-cancerous) growth characterised by an abnormal mixture of cells and tissues native to the specific anatomical location where it develops, a type of swelling that generates seizure activity affecting the pathways involved in laughter.

Gelastic seizures, also known as laughter seizures, were first described by Armand Trousseau, a 19th-century French physician credited with seminal discoveries that advanced the field of medicine.

He described a patient who had an unusual episode of vertigo and jerking bursts of laughter during a routine clinic visit. When Trousseau inquired about the reason for the laughter, the patient was taken aback because he was not aware of it during the spell. Trousseau used the term 'epileptic vertigo' for any transient strange phenomena such as giddiness, astonishment, ecstasy ... fit of absence, which he equated as 'identical in nature with violent convulsions'.

As many as there are functions of the brain, and as complex as the wiring of this wonderful organ that is the control unit of human life, it emanates varied manifestations of electrical abnormality in the form of seizures.

From uncontrolled crying, vomiting, episodes of blindness, fits of rage or madness, bursts of panting and breathlessness, epilepsy has many chameleons that must be understood and managed.

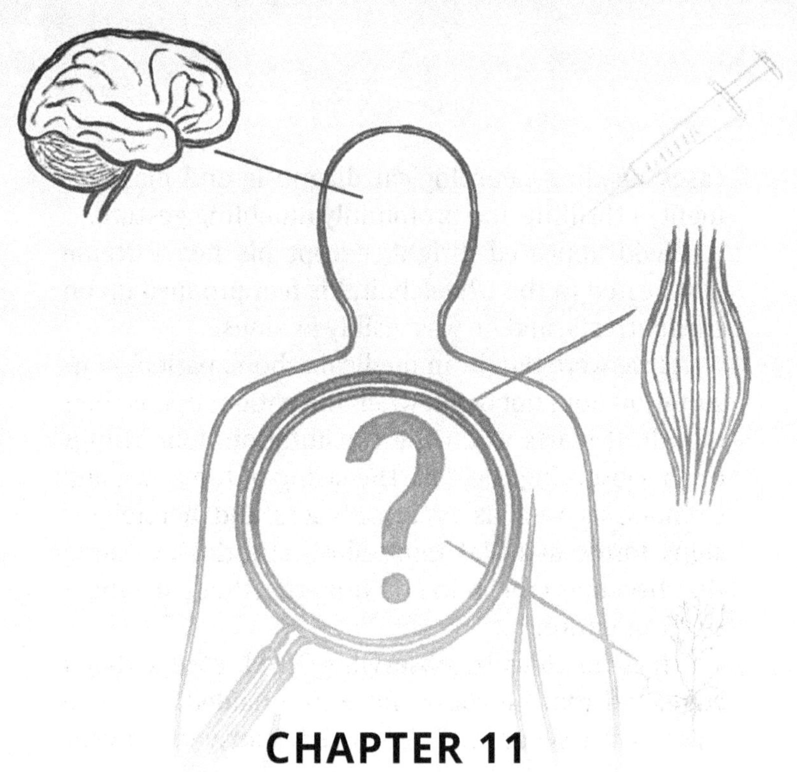

CHAPTER 11

WHERE IS THE PROBLEM?

DAVID ENTERED MY OFFICE IN a wheelchair, his young wife pushing him, both clearly overwhelmed by the turn of events.

He was referred to me by a senior colleague, a medical oncologist. Even before branching into neurology, my training in neuroanatomy and my keen interest in the neurosciences marked me out as a budding neurologist among my peers. They referred to me any cases needing neurological diagnosis and management, a thrilling and profoundly humbling gesture.

David appeared alright, except his heavy frame was nested in the wheelchair, his feet propped up on the footrests, and he was visibly anxious.

As we were taught in medical school, patient consultation does not begin when the patient opens their mouth. It starts when the consultation door swings open. Observing the gait, the swing of the arms, and tremors, as well as breathlessness and hemiplegic signs, forms an initial impression in the doctor's mind that becomes crucial in stitching together a diagnostic formulation.

I had no clues by observing David, except that I could tell that he could not walk unaided. Maybe a spinal cord syndrome? A stroke? Transverse myelitis? Multiple sclerosis? It is not uncommon for ideas to rush through my brain even before I know what I'm dealing with. I find these ideas revelatory, as they facilitate further questioning of the patient and help rule out important differential diagnoses.

His mental faculties were intact. He went on to describe two years of suffering, which started with severe pain in the lower limbs that would ascend to the lower back and the trunk. He described the pains as sharp, lancinating, electric-shock-like. He felt as if he was being quartered with sharp nails. They would come in a crescendo and suddenly disappear. He bought over-the-counter analgesics and decided to wait it out.

The pattern changed to numbness of the upper and lower limbs. So severe was the numbness that he thought he could not feel where his legs were at night. In the mornings, the numbness disappeared, and with it, any urge to seek medical attention.

Over the past four months, he had started to realise that his gait was becoming unsteady. He would get off balance and topple over, even when a thread caught his foot. Walking in the dark became particularly difficult. He would spread his legs widely to maintain balance.

He had finally decided to seek care when he could no longer walk. His legs were weak, and he had completely lost body balance. He now depended on his wife to assist him with visiting the toilet, shower, and moving from one room to another.

A more concerning occurrence was his inability to control his urination and bowel movements. He would feel his bladder full, but by the time he called his wife, he had emptied it. It left him distraught and ashamed. Lately, he had noticed a stool leak before he reached the toilet.

David came from a community where a man must appear stoic, mysterious, and in control of things. A man must not even be known to defecate. His life was now laid bare.

I asked a few more questions to get more clarity. Was there any trauma to the back? Absolutely none, he replied.

Did he take alcohol, smoke cigarettes, or puff marijuana? Yes, he had experimented with alcohol 15 years before, but stopped on his own.

Was there a blurring of vision and dizziness? He answered in the negative.

I turned to the wife.

"Has David experienced any episodes of confusion?"

"Yes, doctor. Two weeks ago, I noticed he was shouting and talking nonsensical things. He accused some unseen people of trying to kill him."

"Have you noticed any loss of consciousness, jerky movements, frothing of the mouth, or any symptoms of *kifafa*?" I ploughed on.

"I have not noticed any of those."

"Is there anyone in his family, a brother, sister, parent, or close cousin who has ever been paralysed or bedridden?"

She rolled her eyes and moved her head around in deep thought. There was none she could recall.

Thoughts were racing through my mind as I picked up my neurology instruments, including the reflex hammer, pin, cotton wool, pen torch, and monofilament.

Just where was the problem?

Localising the problem has been touted as the Holy Grail of diagnosis in neurology. It is better to know *where* the problem is before knowing *what* the problem is. The former narrows the diagnostic process, making it more cost-effective and saving the patient time and potentially even their life.

Jean-Martin Charcot, the father of neurology whose contributions to this field laid the strong foundations for training, is often credited with teaching anatomical localisation. His training as a pathologist, before taking up a clinical position as a neurologist, enabled him to correlate his clinical findings among patients with autopsy results.

Charcot was an avowed, eccentric artist who did not follow the established patterns of his contemporaries. He loved to draw. He had an excellent visual memory and could remember thousands of artistic works and drawings. Perhaps this visual memory imbued him with the extraordinary gift of visualising the complex nervous system and pinpointing the anatomical diagnosis of a neurological presentation.

His legendary Tuesday lessons and case presentations at La Salpêtrière Hospital in France earned him professional acclaim and established him as the leading neurologist of the 19th Century.

When a patient presents with weakness, the clinician must consider the entire neuroaxis and correlate the patient's history and physical examination findings to identify the problem. Even in an era where CT scans and MRI imaging are widely available, this age-old clinical trick remains effective.

The problem could be located in the brain, the spinal cord, the anterior horn cells of the spinal cord, the spinal nerves, the peripheral nerves, the muscles, or the neuromuscular junction. The doctor must pinpoint the most likely location of the weakness and narrow it down with relevant investigations.

When a criminal strikes an estate in a big city, the police will not place the entire city in a lockdown. They don't have the resources to scan the entire metropolis looking for a single human being. They must use a formula, guided by basic principles. Where have past thugs been found? What do the cameras show? Which language did the thug speak? How did he appear? Was he alone, or did he have accomplices? Did he have a mobile phone?

Using these leads, they narrow down the search area and then deploy resources wisely, from undercover operatives to informers and uniformed police. Undercover operatives may decide to frequent pubs in the area of interest and attempt to detect any changes in the drinking habits of patrons. Someone who only takes a bottle of cheap beer and suddenly asks for an expensive beer while displaying unusual generosity and extravagance becomes a suspect.

In Kenya, an MRI scan costs anywhere between 20,000 and 40,000 shillings, depending on the area of the body being scanned. I see migraine patients being forced to do MRI scans of the brain, and I feel their pain.

I once reviewed a 27-year-old gentleman who had a sudden onset of weakness in his upper and lower limbs. His head was normal, and he talked like a parrot. Yet, he had already done a CT scan of the head, and when it did not yield anything, he had been forced to do an MRI of the brain. By the time he saw me, he was exhausted financially. A simple neurological examination localised the problem in the cervical spinal cord. Our only problem was that we needed an MRI of the spinal cord, which he could barely afford.

Although dismissed as 'a freak show' and 'academic showmanship', thorough history and clinical examination in a neurological setting can save money and eventually save lives.

David had poorly contracting pupils, what we call Argyll-Robertson pupils. He had loss of pain on pin-prick in the feet and legs and loss of vibration sense. He could not tell the position of his big toe when I flexed it at its joint, signifying proprioceptive deficiency. We helped him stand. On closing his eyes, he tumbled backwards. He tried to walk, but he shuffled his legs and came crashing down before we could catch him.

I localised his abnormality to the dorsal nerves of the spinal cord and the posterior columns of the spinal cord. This brought relief to my tensed body. He was unable to undergo an MRI scan of the back. However, having narrowed down to the area of interest, it was easy to formulate the differentials. Having formulated the possible differentials, I went for the cheapest tests he could afford.

His syphilis test came positive.

Throughout my undergraduate, graduate and post-graduate studies, I have read about the stages of syphilis, but this was the first time I was coming face to face with tabes dorsalis, a form of neurosyphilis.

Syphilis was, for a long time, a great tormentor of humanity, responsible for paralysis, insanity, psychosis, and untold deaths. The discovery of antibiotics and the inadvertent use of these drugs sent the disease into obscurity. But it did not die completely.

David took a one-month course of doxycycline, a cheap antibiotic. The next time I saw him, he was walking on his own. He still experienced slight gait instability and numbness in his feet, but his progress was evident. I felt a sense of victory and pride in being a doctor with a strong emphasis on anatomy.

But I have seen worse cases of failure to answer the question, where is the problem?

I was a senior resident in internal medicine at the University of Nairobi, rotating in Ward 7B of Kenyatta National Hospital, where neurology consultants would see patients. Requests for consults would come from all floors within the hospital, and it was the work of the senior resident to see those patients and escalate to the consultant whenever needed.

Catherine, a 32-year-old lady, had been admitted to the gynaecology ward, having been referred from Eastern Kenya. She had delivered a live female infant, her first child, who had developed breathing problems immediately after birth. Resuscitation was attempted, but the baby did not survive.

She was admitted because, in addition to losing her baby, she had bouts of weakness, which left her unable to walk. She spotted a big gap in her upper jaw, evidence of a fall she had sustained, which left her with a diastema.

It had been a torrid three years of seeking help without improvement. She had performed CT scans of the brain and the entire spine. When they did not yield anything, she was advised to undergo MRI scans of the brain and the spine. They were normal.

These extensive investigations worsened her precarious situation. Her husband was a menial construction worker, earning less than five hundred shillings per day. She survived by borrowing from relatives. Of late, relatives had started avoiding her. She was not getting any better. They were tired.

"They think I'm bewitched, Daktari," She told me as I scanned her file, which had scant details.

After delivery, her weakness had worsened, prompting the referral that landed her in ward 1D of Kenyatta National Hospital.

I questioned her on the pattern of weakness. Was it sudden in onset? For three years, was it getting better or worsening? Did she experience pain? Was the weakness variable, better in the morning and worsening with increased activity?

I caught a stranglehold.

She had a weakness that worsened with increased activity. Her eyes drooped as the day progressed. Whenever she started experiencing diplopia (double vision), she would shut her eyes for a short time, after which her vision would improve.

Spot diagnoses are not encouraged in medicine, but that day, I was overjoyed as I made a spot diagnosis of myasthenia gravis, a chronic autoimmune disorder causing fluctuating muscle weakness, often affecting the eyes, face, and throat, with symptoms worsening with activity and improving with rest. I explored further—she had no difficulty breathing and no difficulty swallowing, danger signs that would have prompted intensive care management.

Myasthenia gravis is a rare condition in which the body produces antibodies that interfere with the communication between muscles and nerves. Acetylcholine, a chemical neurotransmitter, sends messages between muscles and nerves. It is supposed to dock into receptors that trigger muscle contraction. In this condition, antibodies attack acetylcholine receptors, rendering the neurotransmitter inefficient. A patient will feel weaker as activity intensifies because the few remaining receptors are saturated.

A pregnant mother with myasthenia gravis will transmit the antibodies to the foetus through the placenta. At birth, the baby can suffer a fatal myasthenic crisis occasioned by severe respiratory distress. This is called neonatal myasthenia gravis, which is what probably happened with Catherine and her newborn daughter.

Her case, which I sympathised with, spurred me to undertake retrospective research on myasthenia gravis at the Kenyatta National Hospital. I studied the socio-demographic characteristics of the patients, the time between the onset of symptoms and diagnosis, the major clinical features, and survival over a 10-year period. During my literature review, the only studies on myasthenia gravis conducted in Kenya were two case series, one in 1956 by Dr J R Harries, published in the East African Medical Journal, and another in 1969, also by Dr Harries, published in the Transactions of the Royal Society of Tropical Medicine and Hygiene.

Around 50 patients were treated for myasthenia gravis in the hospital between 2008 and 2017. The majority had ocular symptoms characterised by double vision and drooping of the eyelids. I published my findings to inform my colleagues and future generations that this condition exists and requires early diagnosis.

Sadly, it took three and a half years, on average, from the onset of symptoms to a definitive diagnosis. That is the cost of not asking: Where is the problem?

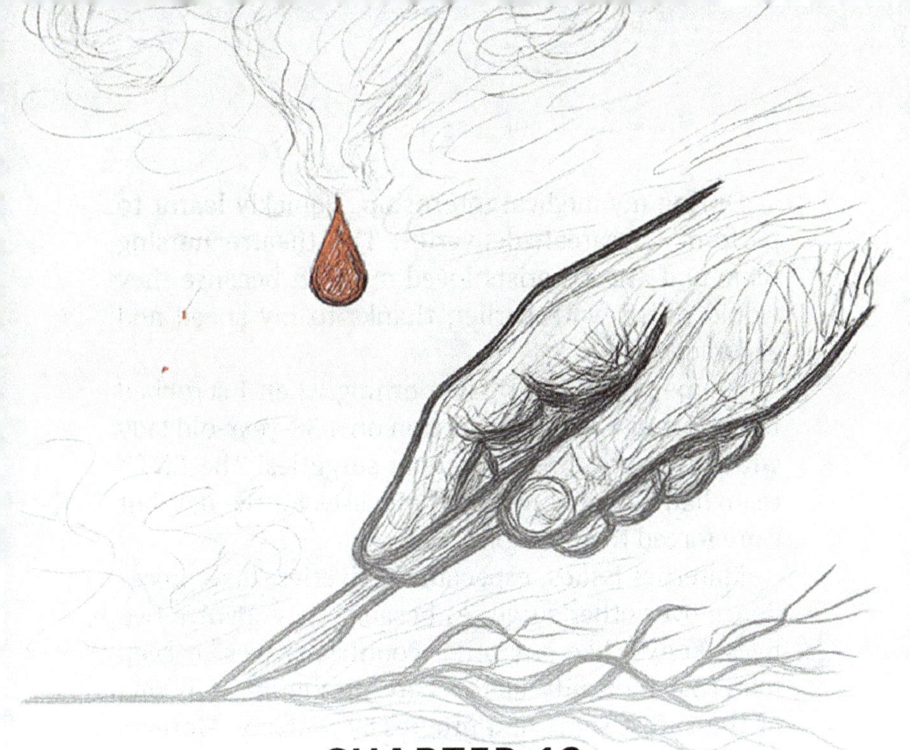

CHAPTER 12

BEYOND EXPECTATIONS

THERE IS NO HEROISM IN medicine. The complexity of the human body, with its integrated networks, makes doctors mere chaperones and cheerleaders in a complicated orchestra, for which they have no control. Any doctor who has practised medicine has been humbled, humiliated, and depressed by medical situations that seemed easy and straightforward but spiralled out of their grasp.

During my medical internship, I quickly learnt to perform Caesarean deliveries. The theatre nursing team and anaesthetists loved my shift because they would finish work earlier, thanks to my speed and accuracy.

I remember one Friday morning when I scrubbed to perform a Caesarean section on a 38-year-old lady with three previous Caesarean surgeries. The ENT[16] team had already lined up their cases for the day, but were forced to give room.

Maternal issues, especially deliveries, take precedence over other surgeries because they involve two lives. Kenya, like any other country, strives to keep maternal mortality at the bare minimum. It is one of the surest signs of a progressive society. Mothers dying while giving life is now ranked among the most unfortunate markers of the backwardness of society.

I gleefully cleaned the patient's suprapubic area as the ENT team watched from a distance. I remember boasting that the longest I would keep them waiting was 15 minutes.

On opening the anterior abdominal wall, I met a chaotic peritoneal cavity. There were thick adhesions, with scar tissue intervening between the uterus and the peritoneum. I was, for once, lost on where I was. Exteriorising the uterus for a quick incision and removal of the baby proved a difficult job.

---

[16] A group of medical professionals specializing in the diagnosis and treatment of ear, nose, and throat (ENT) conditions, also known as otorhinolaryngology.

As I tried in vain to navigate the unfamiliar territory, the ENT senior consultant noticed my predicament and quickly scrubbed, saving me from imminent despair.

"Don't worry. Medicine has to humble you at one point," said Dr Kamanda, the ENT surgeon.

"Sometimes we open up body cavities thinking the normal anatomy is preserved, only to find ourselves in a dense forest where we can't distinguish the blood vessels from other structures," he encouraged.

My bravado was borne out of inexperience. As I have gained experience, so have I encountered many mishaps, not entirely of my own making. I have since learnt not to label any procedure as simple or straightforward.

Some of these simple procedures gone awry are the genesis of malpractice lawsuits that lead to hefty fines and even blacklisting from the roll of doctors. Removal of a simple lipoma can result in ligation of an important vessel, which can be fatal.

I have encountered situations that have tested my belief in some of the ethical principles of medicine, although I strive to do what is right by these principles.

I once quietly processed a certain woman for an MVA and told the accompanying nurse that this was a simple procedure which should take a few minutes. The MVA room was under renovation. We had to use the main theatre for this procedure, which usually took 15 to 20 minutes.

After a few cycles of suctioning, I noted with alarm that the bleeding didn't seem to subside. The sign that all products of conception have been evacuated is when the aspirator evacuates bubbles and when vaginal bleeding stops.

Yet, the more I suctioned, the more blood came out in clots. I stopped to check if the bleeding had subsided. I saw an actively distending abdomen. I aspirated again, evacuating huge clots.

I had the nurse check the patient's conjunctivae for anaemia. She was very pale. We needed a blood transfusion. I called for grouping and cross-matching. Luckily, there were two pints of her blood type in the blood bank. We started administering transfusions as I continued aspirating.

The beauty of medicine sometimes lies in its hierarchy. Unless you are perched at the top, there's always someone senior to call upon when faced with uncertainty. I asked the nurse to call the senior medical officer, who was second on call after me.

He was one of the committed types. Within a few minutes, he was gloved and performing quick sequences of aspiration. The clots kept coming out.

Our professor in paediatrics, the late Professor Rachel Musoke, was respected and feared by everybody within her department. The fear came from her apparent inability to be satisfied with the answers given in an examination.

"What is the cause of the fever in this baby?" She would ask a scared medical student.

Thinking it was an easy question, the hapless student would quickly blurt out the common causes of fever: upper respiratory tract infection, pneumonia, tuberculosis, malaria, pain, and meningitis until he would reach a dead end.

Seemingly unsatisfied, she would ask, "What else?"

She would go on and on, squeezing the last drop of information from the stuttering medical student until the student could speak no more.

Then, as if wringing dry the student, she would remark, "There is something more you've not mentioned." The student would scratch his head, but nothing would be forthcoming.

When I qualified, knowing that I was now off her hook, I once waylaid her outside the Department of Paediatrics. She looked calm and humble.

"Greetings, Prof. May I ask you a question?"

"Sure, go right ahead?" She said, with a characteristic Ugandan inflexion that was unmistakable whenever she spoke. She was a simple lady with neat, grey hair that she liked to tie in a single ponytail at the back of her head. She drove the smallest car in the medical school. But her presence was commanding, and respect and honour preceded her.

"I wish to know why you like asking 'what else?' to medical students even when it is clear they have nothing else to say." I was breathless, shocked by my own bravery in questioning a professor at a time when many preferred to avoid them.

"It is simple, Bundi. When you become a doctor, even when things seem obvious, form a habit of asking yourself if anything else is the issue. It will save you and perhaps save the patient's life."

I stood still to inhale the wisdom she had oozed.

"Understood?" She asked.

"Yes, Prof. Thanks so much," I answered.

"Very well. Go and become the best doctor possible," she said as she made for the wards.

I felt as if I were in a dream. Here was an avowed, simple yet profound formula expounded by the seemingly simple yet erudite and respected professor of paediatrics.

In the cold theatre, as we performed the MVA and tried to save this life, I remembered Prof Musoke's words.

"What else could we be dealing with?" I asked the senior medical officer as he worked on the MVA, sweat forming on his brow.

"What else can it be? Can't you see these are products of conception?" He seemed exasperated at not being able to stem the bleeding despite the frantic efforts.

Two hours later, one pint of blood was transfused, and we were on the verge of giving up. Yet the bleeding didn't stop. If we didn't act decisively, we were going to lose a life.

We made a distress call to the gynaecologist. He thought we had not evacuated all the products of conception, hence the uterus could not contract.

After another 20 minutes of trying, we called him again, this time in desperation. In our efforts to save a life, we were committing a medical error.

The society will frown on medical errors, but doctors and nurses will tell you that medical errors arise from genuine effort. Sometimes errors occur due to omission when a healthcare worker fails to perform a necessary action, either because of a lack of information, insufficient resources, or outright ignorance. These omissions and commissions constitute the bulk of medical errors. However, some errors can't be excused, such as refusing to attend to a patient, attending to a patient when drunk and causing death or injury, overcharging patients, and unnecessary investigations and procedures. This category arises out of laziness, corruption, and poor workmanship. In either category, the doctor stands accused until they can prove they have put in genuine effort, guided by sound science and utilising available resources.

When the gynaecologist came, he also thought we had inadequately evacuated the products of conception. He took the MVA tube and plunger and energetically aspirated. He stopped to look at the aspirate. No doubt they looked like products of conception.

After three rounds of aspiration, the colour of the aspirate changed, and we knew we had entered uncharted territory. The brownish, smelly aspirate was faecal matter. In our spirited efforts, we had breached the uterine wall, which had perhaps been injured by instrumentation during the illegal abortion. We had entered the gut and aspirated faecal matter.

As the second pint of blood ran, we performed an emergency laparotomy[17] for a subtotal hysterectomy (removal of the uterus).

---

[17] A surgical procedure involving a large incision in the abdomen to allow access to the abdominal cavity for examination and treatment of various conditions, including exploring the cause of abdominal pain or addressing specific problems like organ removal or repair.

In a medical field with fine boundaries, we had breached the gynaecological boundary into the surgical field. It was the surgeon's duty to repair the torn gut. He lived over 100 kilometres away. An ambulance was scrambled to pick him up.

By the time the surgeon arrived in the wee hours of the morning, we had removed the uterus. We found a spouting vessel in the junction between the cervix and the uterus. It seems she had been injured in the backstreet clinic where she sought abortion services. This is the *what else* of why bleeding could not stop despite the spirited aspiration.

The surgeon methodically examined the gut and found a perforation in the sigmoid colon, a portion of the large intestine. He performed a thorough washout of the abdominal cavity and then fashioned a colostomy, an opening on the skin of the abdomen, to remove stool. This stool diversion would remain in place for eight weeks until the gut healed, and then another operation would be performed to repair it.

It was 8:00 AM in the morning when we left the theatre, sore and hungry but with loads of lessons in our heads.

The lady's recovery took a protracted course as she battled sepsis, a life-threatening medical emergency caused by the body's extreme response to an infection, causing the immune system to overreact and damage its own tissues and organs. She had bouts of fevers, confusion, and mild kidney failure.

The following week, the husband visited her and asked to speak to me. Perhaps because she was confused, I committed a cardinal sin of explaining to the husband what we had done and her progress.

I saw him bite his lower lip in anger and exasperation.

"How can she be pregnant? I have been in South Africa for the last eight months and just caught an emergency flight to Kenya when I heard she was sick." He paused. "Anyway, let her get well. We shall sort out this problem." He said as he walked out in a huff.

She left the hospital after two weeks. She had lost her uterus and, most likely, her marriage.

What seemed a minor procedure had swelled into a gynaecological and surgical operation and had opened wounds, physical and marital wounds that would fester for years to come.

Nothing in medicine is as simple as it seems.

CHAPTER 13

ON DEATH AND DYING

"TURN TO YOUR NEIGHBOUR AND ask him or her how they would like to die."

These words from our bishop during a sermon series on death and dying cut through my heart like a searing knife through butter. We don't like to imagine our own mortality. The average person will wish to live for over 120 years until they are no longer in control of their own lives and become like babies all over again.

Yet, only two things join humanity—birth and death. We are all conceived through pretty much the same processes, which involve the union of ovum and sperm and the formation of a zygote. How we spend our lives may be a factor of where we are born, who gave birth to us, and the circumstances we find ourselves in. But eventually, whether you spend your life walking on gold or walking on hot coal, death will come calling.

One of the most difficult tasks I perform is escorting patients through their mortality. We like to think that the work of a doctor is only to treat, but it involves, in large part, holding the hands of patients in their final days and standing with relatives during these anxious, eye-opening, and often heart-breaking moments.

After that statement by the bishop, I found myself thinking about how I would like to die: Sudden, painless death? Sleep and not wake up? At what age?

The answers to these questions will remain hidden from our consciousness unless we wish to end our lives ourselves. Very few people have the option of determining what their expiry will look like.

I have stood with patients facing a grim diagnosis, who have, at best, a few weeks to months to die. I have also walked with relatives of a patient in a coma in the intensive care unit, whose life hangs in the balance and can't make their own decisions.

I don't know whether it's a privilege or a curse to have a revelation of one's mortality.

One of the seminal works of a patient walking the path to their death is *When Breath Becomes Air* by Dr

Paul Kalanithi. What makes his journey all the more revealing is that he is a neurosurgical chief resident whose life in the noble profession is just about to take off. Then it happens. Faced with an unexpected diagnosis of Stage 4 lung cancer at the tender age of 36, he is forced to come to terms with his mortality. 'Before this diagnosis, I knew I would die, only I didn't know when. After this diagnosis, nothing much changed. I knew I would die, but I didn't know when. Only that this time, I knew that I had to focus on what mattered to me'. He writes of his mental turmoil upon this diagnosis.

Oliver Sacks, an American neurologist, writes about his impending death after an ocular melanoma that had been in control for over 10 years metastasised to his liver. 'It is up to me now to choose how to live out the months that remain to me. I have to live in the richest, deepest, most productive way I can ... Over the last few days, I have been able to see my life as from a great altitude, as a sort of landscape, and with a deepening sense of the connection of all its parts. This does not mean I am finished with life. On the contrary, I feel intensely alive, and I want and hope in the time that remains to deepen my friendships, to say farewell to those I love, to write more, to travel if I have the strength, to achieve new levels of understanding and insight'.

No one teaches doctors or physicians, whether in medical school or residency, the enormity of death. Only when faced with a dying patient do you truly understand the beauty of life. Some lessons can't be delivered in a theory class until they are lived.

"*Daktari,* how long do I have to live?"

I have faced this question time and again. I will never tell a patient that death is imminent, not at least when they are in control of their mental faculties. In essence, I follow the basic rules of vagueness expounded by Dr Paul Kalanithi—be honest about the prognosis but always leave room for hope. Be vague but accurate: days to weeks, a few weeks to months, and months to years.

A few years ago, I saw a 48-year-old man with severe respiratory distress and fatigue on the slightest exertion. The short walk from the waiting area to my office left him struggling for breath, his words dispersed in broken sentences. I asked him how long he had been sick. He had experienced symptoms for three months.

As he lay on the bed for examination, the thoughts that ran through my mind were that he was suffering from heart failure. Yet he had no obvious risk factors.

I placed a stethoscope on his chest. His breath sounds were audible, apart from some bronchial sounds on the left apex. His cardiac sounds were muffled. A sweep echocardiogram revealed a massive pericardial effusion. I admitted him for pericardiocentesis, a procedure where we insert a tube at the xiphisternum (the breast bone at the lower tip). We drained over 500 millilitres of pericardial fluid. He was greatly relieved.

On further evaluation, we found a tumour on the apex of the left lung. As we were preparing him for an image-guided biopsy to determine the type of tumour, he complained of a severe headache. A CT scan of the brain demonstrated a metastatic deposit in the frontal lobe of the brain.

Lung cancer accounts for the highest cancer mortality worldwide, and survival after diagnosis of metastatic lung cancer is usually estimated at three to six months. Yet, the human body is complex; most statistical estimates fail to account for the unique attributes of individuals.

I discussed with him the grim diagnosis. When he asked about his chances of survival, I avoided the discussion. It is now five years, and after cycles of chemotherapy, radiotherapy, and targeted molecular therapy, he has been tumour-free for three years.

In his book, Dr Paul Kalanithi wonders why physicians, faced with patients with grim diagnoses, obfuscate so much, yet they have so much information. It is due to the uncertainty in the medical sciences. You can't compare human life with what engineers do when they measure roads, bridges, and buildings. It is much more complicated due to the biochemical, physiological, and anatomical nuances, as well as the psychological input that the individual injects into their own body.

A few years ago, I was asked by the family of a 55-year-old lady to take care of her in the intensive care unit. Her medical history went like this: she was hypertensive for five years and diabetic for two years; she was relatively well-controlled and compliant with medications and her doctor's appointments. A day before admission into the ICU, she complained of upper abdominal pain and had one episode of vomiting. Thinking it was gastritis, the husband bought her omeprazole. The pain initially seemed to subside, but then recurred at night. He rushed her to a nearby hospital. The doctor on duty advised on admission. He left her stable and promised to see her the following day.

Early in the morning, he was called and informed that the lady's condition had deteriorated. He rushed to the hospital, only to find her in a coma. Nobody in the hospital could explain what had happened and when it happened, but the nurse doing the early morning checks found her unresponsive.

She was rushed to the ICU, intubated, and put on ventilatory support.

A reconstruction of the sequence of events revealed that she had suffered a myocardial infarction (heart attack), which had been heralded by abdominal pain. In the hospital, this suspicion was not entertained, and no treatment was offered for this. She probably had gone on to suffer a cardiac arrest and subsequent hypoxic damage (lack of oxygen) to the brain.

As I looked at her in the ICU, I could not tell how long the cardiac arrest lasted. Brain cells will mostly be irreversibly damaged when there's insufficient oxygen for more than four minutes. Her pupils were dilated, fixed, and unreactive to light.

The anxious family huddled in the conference room, awaiting a word from me. I could hear the soft sobs of her daughter among the drowning din, beeps and ringing of the ICU machines.

Accompanied by the nurse, we sat for a family conference. This is usually a highly emotional, difficult meeting where the doctor will lay bare the facts about the patient and throw the ball to the family for the final decision. From my experience, few families are ready to make a decision, and they will insist that the doctor make the decision.

During family conferences, I always start by introducing myself and the nurse. I ask family members to introduce themselves and explain their relationship to the patient. I will then describe in detail the patient's history, the findings from the examination and tests performed, and the progress made so far. I find that this helps ease the tension and allows for more productive discussions. It also serves as a buffer in case I'm about to deliver devastating news.

"Whereas Mum's vital signs are stable, we don't know for how long her brain lacked oxygen. We, therefore, don't know whether she will ever wake up from her coma. And if she ever wakes up, there's no guarantee she will ever function independently. At best, I estimate that in the unlikely event she wakes up, she will be bedridden for the rest of her life." I delivered the conclusion, tinged with vagueness.

The husband was the first to speak.

"*Daktari,* because I'm the one who lives with my wife, I have a request to make. Please tell me if she will ever walk again!" He asked.

"I may not be 100 per cent sure, but I think she will never walk again," I replied.

Turning to the children and the other relatives, he said with finality, "I want my wife whole and healthy. If this is not medically possible, she would rather rest in peace."

I marvelled at his bravery. I looked at the sons and daughters. They seemed lost in their own thoughts. I advised that they discuss as a family whether they were willing to sign advance orders against resuscitation or were willing for de-escalation to comfort care.

Later that day, they opted for minimal comfort care and even demanded that she be extubated. The nurses in the unit were in shock; this was the first case they had seen where a spouse was unwilling to cling to fading hope. I performed the extubation but did not linger long in the ICU. She passed on quietly a few hours later.

I knew that her death would have been protracted. I remembered my bishop's sermon on how I would like to die. I'm sure nobody would like to have a protracted struggle with death on the ventilator machine for several weeks or months, even when all evidence points to the inevitability of death.

Our relationship with death also stems from our cultural backgrounds and religion. Some cultures have a mortal fear of death and the dead, while others have a love affair with the dead. They take death as a rite of passage that should be celebrated.

"I want to be mourned properly when I die," I remember one colleague telling me.

"How would you like to be mourned? For how long?" I asked him.

"I want my people to feel they mourned me, spent time with my body, cried, sang, danced, ululated, and performed all rites that will make them satisfied when I'm buried," he said.

We were driving in the hospital van along Langata Road in Nairobi on a cold July morning when we reached the Langata Cemetery. Our driver requested that we enter the cemetery and wait for him to mourn 'a little' with friends who were burying a relative in the cemetery. We asked about his relationship with the dead person. He apparently did not know him, but the dead was a friend of his cousin.

No sooner had he stepped out of the van than he dramatically rolled on the ground and broke into screams and a traditional dirge. We could barely recognise the man we knew so well. He sent wails and screams that pierced our hearts.

He joined a group of mourners who were pacing up and down, beating themselves, and wailing. After what seemed like 30 minutes, he dusted himself and returned to the van. Almost immediately, he was back to his normal self, chatty and happy as always. We were shocked by this cultural display, but again, we understood the communal demands on this man. You have to cry even when you don't know the dead. You have to roll on the ground. Death is a ceremony, and mourning must be tailored to herald this unwelcome guest.

While a resident at the Kenyatta National Hospital, I managed a young lady who came with hepatomegaly, a swelling of the liver. Initial tests showed she was HIV positive. A liver biopsy returned a diagnosis of diffuse large B-cell lymphoma, one of the easily treatable and chemosensitive tumours. We had a dilemma because HIV had already immunosuppressed her, but after a multidisciplinary discussion, we elected to start infusions of chemotherapy.

We had barely given two doses when she went down with severe sepsis. We escalated her antibiotics per protocol, but none seemed to work. She was on the verge of death.

As we performed resuscitation, relatives would peek in. Her mother kept asking if she had died. They seemed to be waiting for death. When she eventually slipped off despite resuscitation, I saw relief amidst her relatives, who all remarked that it was God's will that she die.

Perhaps the most difficult mortality to face, whether as a doctor or a relative, is one that comes out of the blue. I have written in an earlier chapter about a jovial lady I performed a bone marrow aspiration on who died suddenly, without warning.

Facing relatives in that instance is not only frightening, it is humbling, humiliating, and unfathomable. I can't count the number of times I have wept with relatives and seen colleagues so heartbroken to the extent that they can't work for many days when this happens.

There's always some little hope, however faint it is, that as a doctor, there's something you should do, you must do, to keep a patient alive. It is the most difficult situation when the doctor gives up. It sends the patient and relatives down the spiral of despair, but ultimately, they must accept the limitations nature has placed on us.

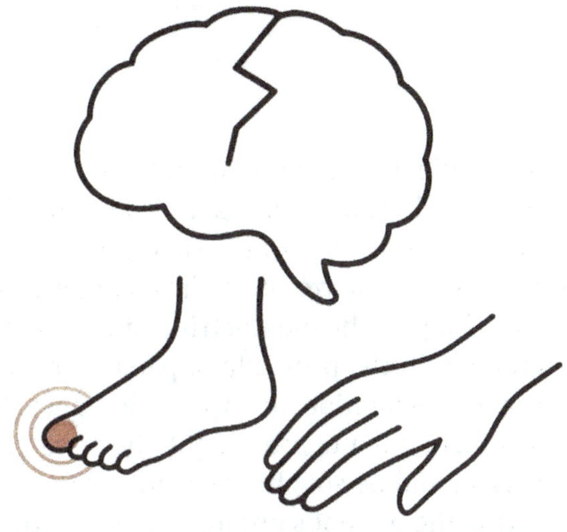

CHAPTER 14

ALL IN THE MIND?

IT IS NOW UNIVERSALLY AGREED by the medical fraternity that dismissing patients with the old cliché 'it is all in the mind' is old-fashioned, inappropriate and perhaps unethical. This phrase has been used for years to refer to symptoms without a structural or known functional basis, now known as Medically Unexplained Symptoms (MUS).

Training of doctors and other healthcare workers is based on the assumption that medical conditions follow a specific pattern and that dysfunction of at least one cell, tissue, organ, or organ system is responsible for disease. When diseases don't follow a known anatomical and physiological, as well as pathological, pattern, they baffle and confuse doctors.

In the complex maze of medical conditions, doctors have clung to the old doctrine of *Occam's Razor,* which hinges on the principle of parsimony and prefers simple explanations over complex ones. Therefore, medical students are taught that one unifying diagnosis should be sought over multiple ones while considering the patient's unique characteristics. Nevertheless, this dictum does not necessarily mean that the more straightforward explanation is more likely correct. It implies that the simplest formulation that explains all the available data and clinical information should be preferred.

More recently, John Hickam (1914–1970) proposed a counterbalance to Occam's Razor, taking into account the unique genetics and epigenetics of individuals, as well as the rapid advancement of medical technology. He famously said, "A patient can have as many diagnoses as he darn well pleases". In *Hickam's dictum,* the law of parsimony is replaced by the law of plenitude, especially in an age where patients live longer and diagnostic technology has rapidly improved.

Is it possible, then, for a patient to have a disease that can't be explained by medical logic but is only explainable by mental changes? Telling a patient that it is all in the mind is essentially a summary dismissal—an indication that either the patient is pretending or that they have the power to control the condition.

I have struggled with this phenomenon for years, both as a medical student and a physician, until I recently sat down to review my own history. I subsequently made a self-diagnosis about a condition I have battled for over 20 years. Only the realisation that this condition was some sort of imbalance in the brain saved me from several trials of medical therapy, surgery, and even possible amputation of my left toe. Through this journey, I learnt that bringing the subconscious to the conscious is a great victory in itself and can save you from pain and suffering.

We have yet to fully understand the brain; it will take centuries. This is the only organ in the body that minds all other organs and, as if by remote control, censors their functions. It is the brain that determines whether the heart beats or not. You subconsciously take gulps of air as if on automatic gear because some brain cells sense subtle changes in the acidity of the blood and trigger you to breathe in and out. The brain is the central processing unit on which almost all body functions depend. With billions of cells making trillions of connections with each other, emitting trillions of signals, this 1-kilogram organ nestled within the skull remains a mystery to be unlocked.

I recently ran a quick survey among a group of physicians on which condition they would wish to have: a stroke or a heart attack—99 per cent of them would prefer to have a heart attack. If you survive the chest pain, you continue life as an intact person, albeit with a few limitations. In the case of a stroke, survival turns you into a completely different person. You are not your legs, face, trunk, lungs—you are your brain. No sooner does it malfunction than your whole essence, beginning with basic functions, interactions, personality, memory stock, and all that you are, comes crumbling down.

Back to my experience.

I was in Form Three in high school when I woke up one day with a mysterious sharp pain in my left big toe. I initially ignored it, thinking I had worn ill-fitting shoes, but the intensity exponentially increased as the days went on. It became so intense that I had to wear open shoes to class.

The frequent visits to the school nurse were of little help. She prescribed various analgesics and graduated up the ladder of strength as my visits increased. There was no swelling of the toe, only a deep, dull ache that made me feel as if the toe was continually boiling.

As I graduated to the final year of high school, the pain continued, as did the use of analgesics. Then, after the Kenya Certificate for Secondary Education (KCSE) examinations in 2002, it vanished as mysteriously as it had appeared.

Throughout my two pre-university years, I did not experience the pain and forgot about it. During this time, I initially worked as an untrained teacher and then as an attachee in a major bank for a year.

I entered medical school hoping for an easier time than I had had in high school. My friends had told me they were free to attend classes and lived in their own rooms with powerful radios and music systems. I was looking forward to these moments of joy. But the first year hit us like a thunderbolt. I found myself struggling to catch up with the pace of information. More annoyingly, the spirit of competition was so intense that almost all the top 100 students in the country in KCSE were now in the same class. If you are used to effortlessly scoring 90% in high school exams, medical school humbles and frustrates you. We had to go on our knees to intercede for the 50% pass mark, without which we could not proceed to the next level. Potentially, you can spend a decade in medical school.

The pressure must have been worse on me, for having been first among equals, I had to prove that my victory was not a random incident. I worked my boots off.

As if on cue, the pain in my left toe resumed, this time with greater ferocity than the initial episode. I limped my way from the main campus of the University of Nairobi to the Chiromo Campus (where the preclinical medical school is located) for most of the year. Whenever I got time, I would visit the university clinic, where various treatments were prescribed. I studied through my pain and suffering and finished my first year of university. The end of the first year was like the release of a pressure valve. It was therapeutic, if not unbelievable.

Again, the pain eased, and I even forgot about it. Two months later, we started our second year of training. Although the pressure was less than in the first year, partly because of getting accustomed to the system, the pain rebounded. The serious medical students of the first year transformed into relaxed and less caring second-year students.

"After all, I don't need a distinction to be a neurosurgeon," my friend would say.

"Even our professors barely scraped through with 52%, and they are thriving in medical practice," we comforted ourselves.

On one visit to the University clinic, I was referred to the orthopaedic clinic in Kenyatta National Hospital. Two senior orthopaedic surgeons reviewed me and came up with two possible differentials for the pain. Either I had an ingrown toenail or gout. They ordered an MRI, which came back normal. The blood tests for gout were negative.

They put me on the minor theatre list for toenail extraction. Heck, I even heard one of them mention possible amputation of the toe.

On the theatre day, I didn't show up. I was afraid.

The pain kept increasing, and I went back to the university clinic. This time, the medical officer sent me to a consultant psychiatrist. He did not explain much but prescribed imipramine (antidepressants). When I told my friends about my prescription, one of them burst out laughing, saying that I was being treated for madness.

I took just one dose and went bonkers. I have realised our bodies handle drugs differently. Some humans can withstand just any drug and walk stoically as if nothing is happening. Others require only a small dose to lose complete control of their network. That's what happened. Just a small dose of imipramine and my mouth went dry like wood. I could barely see. I was groggy. My sleep was punctuated with vivid dreams. I even lapsed into a half-awake dream.

Imipramine belongs to the Tricyclic Antidepressants category of drugs. It treats stress, anxiety, depression, and other functional pains originating from nerves. It is also used to treat functional disorders—conditions without a clear aetiological and anatomical basis. It alters the balance of certain chemicals in the brain, increasing the chemicals that cause happiness, cancel pain and promote sleep.

It was after this debacle that I sat down to analyse my condition. What could be the problem? Will I survive? I had many questions in my mind. I traced the symptoms from my high school days and noted an uncanny pattern—the pain seemed to emerge whenever I was facing mental pressure. It was a clear, surprising pattern.

This discovery brought relief and healing. The pain eased. I stopped visiting the doctor. I stopped my medications.

Still, the pain visits me like an evil angel, but having discovered myself, I know when I feel the pain, I'm subjecting myself to more pressure than necessary. Simple relaxation, breathing exercises and mindfulness usually resolve the pain without the need for analgesia.

I recently shared this with a group of friends, and they teased me that my toe is like a thermostat; it senses the changes in anxiety and stress levels in my brain.

I still can't bring myself to tell a patient blatantly that 'it is all in your mind'. This is dismissive, unkind and inappropriate. I strive to help patients walk through their lives and come to the moment of truth about what is ailing them. Only through self-discovery can a patient understand this condition and commit to healing.

It is, therefore, plausible that the many cases of burning pain, indigestion, loose motions, chest pains, joint pains, headaches, and even fatigue are the manifestations of a battered mind.

It takes a deep understanding of your body to help yourself. Otherwise, you can spend all your wealth and even sell your assets, looking for the elusive magical cure for something that lies within your brain matter.

In simple terms, the subconscious is the elephant that you must get out of the room for real healing to occur.

CHAPTER 15

A MEANINGFUL ENCOUNTER WITH YOUR DOCTOR

THE RELATIONSHIP BETWEEN THE DOCTOR and the patient is often complicated. Almost 70 per cent of the time, the patient holds the key to his problem. The doctor will use the history adduced from the patient and findings on examination to make a clinical impression. The clinical impression will, in turn, inform the next course of action, whether a spot diagnosis has been made or if further investigations are needed. Some diseases must be confirmed by laboratory and imaging investigations, regardless of whether the doctor thinks they have clinched the diagnosis or not.

A patient known to have diabetes, hypertension or a chronic smoker who presents with sudden onset weakness of the right side of the body and loss of speech almost invariably has a stroke. Yet the doctor must order a CT scan of the head to confirm the diagnosis, but most importantly, to differentiate whether the stroke is a bleed in the brain or a blockage of a vessel. This differentiation makes a world of difference because both strokes are treated in tangentially different ways.

Some diagnoses must be treated, whether the confirmatory tests are available or not. A middle-aged lady who comes with sudden onset chest pain and difficulty in breathing and who is suspected to have suffered a pulmonary embolism must be treated even in the absence of the confirmatory test. The rationale here is that, left untreated, the lady might suffer fatal complications. It is reasonable to treat and be proven wrong later by an investigation than not treat and wait for confirmation, by which time you might have no patient to treat.

Sometimes, the patient's narration of the sequence of events and their severity may throw the doctor off-balance and bring untold complications. There's an assumption that the doctor has prophetic powers. A patient gasping for air at the slightest exertion will start narrating some nondescript joint pain. An observant doctor will realise that there's more than what the patient is saying.

Gabriel García Márquez, in his book *Love in the Time of Cholera,* introduces Dr Juvenal Urbino, a highly respected doctor in the fictional town of Macondo. He loves his job as a community doctor and helps combat the ravaging cholera epidemic. Having encountered the nuances of treating patients of all ages, he argues: "Paediatrics is the most honest specialisation because children become sick when, in fact, they are sick, and they cannot communicate with the physician using conventional words but only with concrete symptoms of real diseases. After a certain age, however, adults either have the symptoms without the disease or, what is worse, a serious disease with the symptoms of minor ones."

On the other end of the spectrum, geriatrics[18] will behave almost like children, but the complexity of their bodies and behaviours learned over many years makes their diagnosis a particularly difficult sport for physicians.

I have encountered patients who have erectile dysfunction but will not disclose their problems. They will prefer to go round in circles over many visits. One time, they will feign a stomach upset; next time, they will have a headache or joint pains. After several visits, they may speak as if in parables, hoping you will decode the meaning.

"I don't know what I'm feeling, doctor." One 51-year-old man told me during a visit. "You see,

---

[18] The branch of medicine that deals with the health, care, and diseases of older people (above 65 years).

women of nowadays don't understand our predicaments," he continued.

As a curious listener, I took mental note of that statement.

I decided to do a quick questioning from head to toe: he had non-specific headaches, insomnia, indigestion, and fatigue. However, that did not appear to be the reason for the consultation to me.

"My wife accuses me of infidelity, which is false," he hinted.

"Are you having a problem with your wife?" I asked.

"No."

I prolonged the discussion deliberately, hoping he would open up about poor sexual performance, but he took a circuitous route.

Finally, I decided to ask myself.

"Is there a problem with sexual performance?"

"Yes! In fact, I have been accused of keeping mistresses when my problem is that I can't perform optimally."

As old age approaches, many patients will have more than one condition, often requiring a large number of prescriptions. Doctors are not equipped by training or their own initiative to ask about the mental status or even sexual health of patients.

An 80-year-old man I had seen for three years, who was on management for diabetes, hypertension, arthritis, and gastritis, was started on tamsulosin, a drug that reduces the size of the prostate. This was after he experienced urinary frequency at night and incontinence whenever he felt the urge to pass urine.

He came to the hospital for his routine appointment with his 78-year-old wife.

They looked like a lovely couple. Their body language spoke of a life of love and sharing.

After my routine questioning, I asked the wife if she wanted to add anything to what the man had told me. I usually find women more given to details, and their additions will provide crucial insights into the well-being of their husbands.

"I know you look like our young son or even grandchild, but we shall not fear you," the wife remarked.

"Sure, don't worry. Here, I see and treat everything, and the physical body has no part that is secret to a physician." This was a subtle way of telling them I had seen or dealt with almost any complaint in my journey as a doctor.

"John, tell him!" she deflected to the old man.

I saw them look at each other for an uneasy minute, and then the wife said, "Since John started this drug, tamsulosin, nothing is happening in the house. Nothing at all. He is flat!"

John interjected, "Actually, she accuses me of having a secret arrangement, what they call *mpango wa kando.*"

I felt uneasy discussing this topic with an elderly couple, but I was encouraged that they were open and willing to talk.

Seeing as the visit to the doctor is a golden opportunity to discuss your problem and guide the doctor toward helping you, I have compiled what I think are important tips to assist you. Some people may shrug off the idea that they rarely visit the doctor, but it may not be their choice when the time comes.

WRITE DOWN YOUR PROBLEMS in order of importance or urgency. Try to limit the concerns to three or four major ones. Presenting a list of 15 symptoms to the doctor carries the risk of distracting them and losing focus on what is truly important. If your doctor is good, they should probe for additional symptoms to help them piece together the puzzle.

GO STRAIGHT TO THE POINT. Patients will begin by narrating events that occurred 40 years ago. They will recount their visits to doctors, herbalists, and even healers. In the process, they complain about the mistreatment that has been meted out against them. I have seen patients who start their history by explaining how they went to a major hospital, had scans done, and were given certain medications, but nothing improved. In the process, I interrupt and ask them to state exactly what brought them to me.

Giving proper history is a function of a clear mind. Narrating the sequence of events succinctly helps the doctor focus his mind on the possible differential diagnosis, avoid unnecessary investigations, and save time and money.

Some patients will give proper history, but they come with a fixed mind—they believe they know what their problem is and what triggered it. "My problem began 40 years ago after I was caned by a teacher in primary school." Or, "My problem began two years ago after I took turkey in a function." These fixations serve to imprison the patient's mind and make healing difficult.

BRING A RELATIVE or friend. These help distil the symptoms correctly, especially where the patient may not be aware of what is happening. In conditions like epilepsy, stroke, dementia, and syncope (fainting), the history of a patient may not help much.

I see unaccompanied epileptic patients on their first visit. Apart from knowing that they had a seizure, they will not know how they behaved during the seizure attack, whether there was rolling of the eyes, frothing at the mouth, generalised jerky motor activity or post-event confusion. They will need a witness to corroborate the events. It takes a spouse or partner to disclose ominous symptoms like nocturnal seizures, sleep disorders, bed wetting, snoring, apnoeic attacks, and wheezing.

HAVE A LIST of your current medications. Most patients won't remember the names of their drugs. Some patients describe drugs by their colour. "I'm taking the small brown tablet or the big white tablet" will not help the doctor because many drugs have the same colour.

I once saw an elderly man who frequently visited various hospitals. He would go to the hospital every two weeks for minor complaints. Each time, he did not disclose that he was on medication from another doctor. The result was that he had piled medications of the same class, and he was taking all of them. By the time I saw him, he had moderate kidney failure. I refused to treat him unless he went home and brought all his drugs. I was shocked to see he was on three different non-steroidal anti-inflammatory drugs, four hypertension drugs of the same class, and four proton pump inhibitors (acid drugs) of the same class. This was the cause of his kidney failure. I recommended that we dispose of all the medications and start on a clean slate. However, I was unsure if he would limit himself to a single doctor. Whereas many people are naturally averse to hospitals, there are those who will visit the hospital at the slightest hint of a headache. It is the opposite end of the spectrum and can be more detrimental than advantageous.

DRESS FOR THE OCCASION. Yes, dress for it. A patient with chest pains shouldn't be dressed in a cassock or a tight-fitting dress that takes a long time to remove. A patient with knee pain shouldn't be dressed in tight pants that can't be raised to expose the knees. If you have an abdominal complaint, you should be aware that the doctor will likely want to examine and possibly palpate your abdomen.

I saw a 71-year-old man who reported with severe left-sided chest pains. Naturally, left-sided chest pains evoke fear because that's the location of the heart. The sad bit was that he had been seen in a fairly big hospital. A troponin test [19]had been ordered, with a suspicion of a heart attack. When it came back neg-

---

[19] A test that measures the levels of troponin proteins (troponin I or troponin T) in the blood, which are released when heart muscle is damaged, and is primarily used to diagnose heart attacks or evaluate other causes of heart injury.

ative, they performed a chest CT scan. It didn't show anything.

I asked the old man to shed his heavy clothing. The diagnosis was staring back at me: a herpetic rash running just below the left nipple. I bet the only reason he wasn't examined in the other hospital was his mode of dress. Or maybe I'm playing the devil's advocate?

ASK ABOUT YOUR DIAGNOSIS. Patients go around hospitals seeking medical care, but they will rarely ask what they are being treated for. Some even have had major surgeries, but did not ask what was done and why it was done. While it is the doctor's duty to inform the patient of their diagnosis, it is a higher duty of the body's custodian to demand to know what they are being treated for.

SEEK A SECOND OPINION. A second opinion in medicine brings clarity and helps illuminate issues more effectively. If you are being treated for a condition and are not improving, you have the right to seek a second opinion. Your doctor has a duty to refer you for the opinion. As you do this, be wary of being a hospital or doctor hopper.

Lastly, ADHERE TO THE GIVEN TREATMENT. Some interventions take time to bring the desired effects. I see diabetic patients with sugars of 12, 15 or 17 call after one or two days of new medications, complaining that the drugs are not working. Some will even stop the medications and visit another physician.

Medical interventions can take time to work. Remember to ask your doctor how long it will take before you start seeing noticeable improvement.

Once you visit a doctor, you have entered into a relationship of trust. You need to be primed to benefit maximally while also playing your role properly. After all, medicine, as has been said severally, is an imperfect science. Only through cooperation and openness between the doctor and the patient can the mystery of disease be unravelled and proper management instituted.

CONCLUSION

THIS STORY IS A REFLECTION of the daily struggles of a physician. It illuminates the intricacies and doubts that go through a doctor's mind and presents to you the imperfect science of medicine. Amazingly, the science intended to save lives is the most imperfect, due to the complexity of the human anatomy and physiology, as well as the numerous ways diseases cause changes within this system.

However, the book also provides a historical context of disease, giving the reader some background on where we have come from and what the future portends. The information provided here equips the reader with the knowledge necessary for life-or-death situations, pandemics, and suffering, as well as when preparing for a medical encounter.

Finally, this book is about gratitude. If you have gone through every story, one thing you will realise is how randomly disease strikes. We tend to blame victims, but many diseases arise from random mutations and other predispositions that science has yet to unravel. Out of 10 smokers, only one may get lung cancer. And not necessarily the chain smoker. This randomness should teach us to live in the moment and be grateful for every waking day.

ABOUT THE AUTHOR

DR BUNDI KARAU was the best candidate in Kenya for the Kenya Certificate of Secondary Education (KCSE) in 2002. He obtained a Bachelor of Science (BSc) in Human Anatomy, a Bachelor of Medicine and Bachelor of Surgery (MBChB), a Master of Medicine in Internal Medicine (MMed), and a PhD in Human Anatomy (Neurosciences), all from the University of Nairobi. He later undertook a subspecialist Fellowship in Neurology from St John's Medical College in Bangalore, India.

He has also authored a motivational text for students, *The Journey to Academic Success and Beyond*, which continues to provide valuable insights to students in high school and college.

He currently works as a Senior Lecturer in Internal Medicine at the Kenya Methodist University, an Honorary Consultant Physician at Meru Teaching and Referral Hospital, and Chief Physician and Neurologist at Oregon Health Services. He has conducted medical research, particularly in the field of clinical neurosciences, and has published extensively in this area.

He has served on the boards of various high schools. During his spare time, he motivates high school and college students. In 2023, he was one of *Business Daily's* Top 40 under 40 Men laureates for his excellence in academia, clinical service, and community work.

His hobbies include storytelling, writing, travelling and public speaking.

He lives in Meru with his wife, a consultant paediatrician, paediatric diabetologist, and endocrinologist, and he is blessed with three sons.

www.ingramcontent.com/pod-product-compliance
Lightning Source LLC
LaVergne TN
LVHW020510100826
845148LV00003B/740

* 9 7 8 9 9 1 4 9 4 9 1 8 6 *